D0065449

DIABETES

GENERAL EDITORS

Dale C. Garell, M.D.
Medical Director, California Children Services, Department of Health
  Services, County of Los Angeles
Associate Dean for Curriculum; Clinical Professor, Department of Pediatrics &
  Family Medicine, University of Southern California School of Medicine
Former President, Society for Adolescent Medicine

Solomon H. Snyder, M.D.
Distinguished Service Professor of Neuroscience, Pharmacology, and
  Psychiatry, Johns Hopkins University School of Medicine
Former President, Society for Neuroscience
Albert Lasker Award in Medical Research, 1978

CONSULTING EDITORS

Robert W. Blum, M.D., Ph.D.
Associate Professor, School of Public Health and Department of
  Pediatrics
Director, Adolescent Health Program, University of Minnesota
Consultant, World Health Organization

Charles E. Irwin, Jr., M.D.
Associate Professor of Pediatrics; Director, Division of Adolescent
  Medicine, University of California, San Francisco

Lloyd J. Kolbe, Ph.D.
Chief, Office of School Health & Special Projects, Center for Health
  Promotion & Education, Centers for Disease Control
President, American School Health Association

Jordan J. Popkin
Director, Division of Federal Employee Occupational Health, U.S. Public
  Health Service Region I

Joseph L. Rauh, M.D.
Professor of Pediatrics and Medicine, Adolescent Medicine, Children's
  Hospital Medical Center, Cincinnati
Former President, Society for Adolescent Medicine

THE ENCYCLOPEDIA OF
H E A L T H

MEDICAL DISORDERS
AND THEIR TREATMENT

Dale C. Garell, M.D. • General Editor

DIABETES

Marjorie Little

Introduction by C. Everett Koop, M.D., Sc.D.
former Surgeon General, U.S. Public Health Service

CHELSEA HOUSE PUBLISHERS

New York • Philadelphia

The goal of the ENCYCLOPEDIA OF HEALTH *is to provide general information in the ever-changing areas of physiology, psychology, and related medical issues. The titles in this series are not intended to take the place of the professional advice of a physician or other health care professional.*

ON THE COVER   Color-enhanced electron micrograph of pancreatic cells, magnified 17,500 times. Insulin-secreting beta cells appear green and orange; glucagon-secreting alpha cells appear dark brown.

Chelsea House Publishers
EDITOR-IN-CHIEF   Remmel Nunn
MANAGING EDITOR   Karyn Gullen Browne
COPY CHIEF   Juliann Barbato
PICTURE EDITOR   Adrian G. Allen
ART DIRECTOR   Maria Epes
DEPUTY COPY CHIEF   Mark Rifkin
ASSISTANT ART DIRECTOR   Noreen Romano
MANUFACTURING MANAGER   Gerald Levine
SYSTEMS MANAGER   Lindsey Ottman
PRODUCTION MANAGER   Joseph Romano
PRODUCTION COORDINATOR   Marie Claire Cebrián

The Encyclopedia of Health
SENIOR EDITOR   Jake Goldberg

Staff for DIABETES
COPY EDITOR   Karen Hammonds
EDITORIAL ASSISTANTS   Leigh Hope Wood, Kathleen Dolan
PICTURE RESEARCHER   Villette Harris
SENIOR DESIGNER   Marjorie Zaum

3   5   7   9   8   6   4   2

Library of Congress Cataloging-in-Publication Data

Little, Marjorie
    I. Diabetes/Marjorie Little
        p.   cm.—(The Encyclopedia of Health)
    Includes bibliographical references
    ISBN 0-7910-0061-3
            0-7910-0488-0 (pbk.)
    1. Diabetes—Juvenile Literature [1.Diabetes] I. Title. II. Series.   90-1720
RC660.L57 1990   CIP
616.4'62—dc20   AC

CONTENTS

THE ENCYCLOPEDIA OF
H E A L T H

THE HEALTHY BODY

The Circulatory System
Dental Health
The Digestive System
The Endocrine System
Exercise
Genetics & Heredity
The Human Body: An Overview
Hygiene
The Immune System
Memory & Learning
The Musculoskeletal System
The Nervous System
Nutrition
The Reproductive System
The Respiratory System
The Senses
Speech & Hearing
Sports Medicine
Vision
Vitamins & Minerals

THE LIFE CYCLE

Adolescence
Adulthood
Aging
Childhood
Death & Dying
The Family
Friendship & Love
Pregnancy & Birth

MEDICAL ISSUES

Careers in Health Care
Environmental Health
Folk Medicine
Health Care Delivery
Holistic Medicine
Medical Ethics
Medical Fakes & Frauds
Medical Technology
Medicine & the Law
Occupational Health
Public Health

PYSCHOLOGICAL DISORDERS AND THEIR TREATMENT

Anxiety & Phobias
Child Abuse
Compulsive Behavior
Delinquency & Criminal Behavior
Depression
Diagnosing & Treating Mental Illness
Eating Habits & Disorders
Learning Disabilities
Mental Retardation
Personality Disorders
Schizophrenia
Stress Management
Suicide

MEDICAL DISORDERS AND THEIR TREATMENT

AIDS
Allergies
Alzheimer's Disease
Arthritis
Birth Defects
Cancer
The Common Cold
Diabetes
Emergency Medicine
Gynecological Disorders
Headaches
The Hospital
Kidney Disorders
Medical Diagnosis
The Mind-Body Connection
Mononucleosis and Other Infectious Diseases
Nuclear Medicine
Organ Transplants
Pain
Physical Handicaps
Poisons & Toxins
Prescription & OTC Drugs
Sexually Transmitted Diseases
Skin Disorders
Stroke & Heart Disease
Substance Abuse
Tropical Medicine

PREVENTION
AND
EDUCATION:
THE KEYS
TO GOOD HEALTH

C. Everett Koop, M.D., Sc.D.
former Surgeon General,
U.S. Public Health Service

The issue of health education has received particular attention in recent years because of the presence of AIDS in the news. But our response to this particular tragedy points up a number of broader issues that doctors, public health officials, educators, and the public face. In particular, it points up the necessity for sound health education for citizens of all ages.

Over the past 25 years this country has been able to bring about dramatic declines in the death rates for heart disease, stroke, accidents, and for people under the age of 45, cancer. Today, Americans generally eat better and take better care of themselves than ever before. Thus, with the help of modern science and technology, they have a better chance of surviving serious—even catastrophic—illnesses. That's the good news.

But, like every phonograph record, there's a flip side, and one with special significance for young adults. According to a report issued in 1979 by Dr. Julius Richmond, my predecessor as Surgeon General, Americans aged 15 to 24 had a higher death rate in 1979 than they did 20 years earlier. The causes: violent death and injury, alcohol and drug abuse, unwanted pregnancies, and sexually transmitted diseases. Adolescents are particularly vulnerable because they are beginning to explore their own sexuality and perhaps to experiment with drugs. The need for educating young people is critical, and the price of neglect is high.

Yet even for the population as a whole, our health is still far from what it could be. Why? A 1974 Canadian government report attributed all death and disease to four broad elements: inadequacies in the health care system, behavioral factors or unhealthy life-styles, environmental hazards, and human biological factors.

To be sure, there are diseases that are still beyond the control of even our advanced medical knowledge and techniques. And despite yearnings that are as old as the human race itself, there is no "fountain of youth" to ward off aging and death. Still, there is a solution to many of the problems that undermine sound health. In a word, that solution is prevention. Prevention, which includes health promotion and education, saves lives, improves the quality of life, and in the long run, saves money.

In the United States, organized public health activities and preventive medicine have a long history. Important milestones in this country or foreign breakthroughs adopted in the United States include the improvement of sanitary procedures and the development of pasteurized milk in the late 19th century and the introduction in the mid-20th century of effective vaccines against polio, measles, German measles, mumps, and other once-rampant diseases. Internationally, organized public health efforts began on a wide-scale basis with the International Sanitary Conference of 1851, to which 12 nations sent representatives. The World Health Organization, founded in 1948, continues these efforts under the aegis of the United Nations, with particular emphasis on combating communicable diseases and the training of health care workers.

Despite these accomplishments, much remains to be done in the field of prevention. For too long, we have had a medical care system that is science- and technology-based, focused, essentially, on illness and mortality. It is now patently obvious that both the social and the economic costs of such a system are becoming insupportable.

Implementing prevention—and its corollaries, health education and promotion—is the job of several groups of people.

First, the medical and scientific professions need to continue basic scientific research, and here we are making considerable progress. But increased concern with prevention will also have a decided impact on how primary care doctors practice medicine. With a shift to health-based rather than morbidity-based medicine, the role of the "new physician" will include a healthy dose of patient education.

Second, practitioners of the social and behavioral sciences—psychologists, economists, city planners—along with lawyers, business leaders, and government officials—must solve the practical and ethical dilemmas confronting us: poverty, crime, civil rights, literacy, education, employment, housing, sanitation, environmental protection, health care delivery systems, and so forth. All of these issues affect public health.

Third is the public at large. We'll consider that very important group in a moment.

Fourth, and the linchpin in this effort, is the public health profession— doctors, epidemiologists, teachers—who must harness the professional expertise of the first two groups and the common sense and cooperation of the third, the public. They must define the problems statistically and qualitatively and then help us set priorities for finding the solutions.

To a very large extent, improving those statistics is the responsibility of every individual. So let's consider more specifically what the role of the individual should be and why health education is so important to that role. First, and most obvious, individuals can protect themselves from illness and injury and thus minimize their need for professional medical care. They can eat nutritious food, get adequate exercise, avoid tobacco, alcohol, and drugs, and take prudent steps to avoid accidents. The proverbial "apple a day keeps the doctor away" is not so far from the truth, after all.

Second, individuals should actively participate in their own medical care. They should schedule regular medical and dental checkups. Should they develop an illness or injury, they should know when to treat themselves and when to seek professional help. To gain the maximum benefit from any medical treatment that they do require, individuals must become partners in that treatment. For instance, they should understand the effects and side effects of medications. I counsel young physicians that there is no such thing as too much information when talking with patients. But the corollary is the patient must know enough about the nuts and bolts of the healing process to understand what the doctor is telling him or her. That is at least partially the patient's responsibility.

Education is equally necessary for us to understand the ethical and public policy issues in health care today. Sometimes individuals will encounter these issues in making decisions about their own treatment or that of family members. Other citizens may encounter them as jurors in medical malpractice cases. But we all become involved, indirectly, when we elect our public officials, from school board members to the president. Should surrogate parenting be legal? To what extent is drug testing desirable, legal, or necessary? Should there be public funding for family planning, hospitals, various types of medical research, and other medical care for the indigent? How should we allocate scant technological resources, such as kidney dialysis and organ transplants? What is the proper role of government in protecting the rights of patients?

What are the broad goals of public health in the United States today? In 1980, the Public Health Service issued a report aptly entitled *Promoting Health—Preventing Disease: Objectives for the Nation.* This report expressed its goals in terms of mortality and in terms of intermediate goals in education and health improvement. It identified 15 major concerns: controlling high blood pressure; improving family planning; improving pregnancy care and infant health; increasing the rate of immunization; controlling sexually transmitted diseases; controlling the presence of toxic agents and radiation in the environment; improving occupational safety and health; preventing accidents; promoting water fluoridation and dental health; controlling infectious diseases; decreasing smoking; decreasing alcohol and drug abuse; improving nutrition; promoting physical fitness and exercise; and controlling stress and violent behavior.

For healthy adolescents and young adults (ages 15 to 24), the specific goal was a 20% reduction in deaths, with a special focus on motor vehicle injuries and alcohol and drug abuse. For adults (ages 25 to 64), the aim was 25% fewer deaths, with a concentration on heart attacks, strokes, and cancers.

Smoking is perhaps the best example of how individual behavior can have a direct impact on health. Today, cigarette smoking is recognized as the single most important preventable cause of death in our society. It is responsible for more cancers and more cancer deaths than any other known agent; is a prime risk factor for heart and blood vessel disease, chronic bronchitis, and emphysema; and is a frequent cause of complications in pregnancies and of babies born prematurely, underweight, or with potentially fatal respiratory and cardiovascular problems.

Since the release of the Surgeon General's first report on smoking in 1964, the proportion of adult smokers has declined substantially, from 43% in 1965 to 30.5% in 1985. Since 1965, 37 million people have quit smoking. Although there is still much work to be done if we are to become a "smoke-free society," it is heartening to note that public health and public education efforts—such as warnings on cigarette packages and bans on broadcast advertising—have already had significant effects.

In 1835, Alexis de Tocqueville, a French visitor to America, wrote, "In America the passion for physical well-being is general." Today, as then, health and fitness are front-page items. But with the greater scientific and technological resources now available to us, we are in a far stronger position to make good health care available to everyone. And with the greater technological threats to us as we approach the 21st century, the need to do so is more urgent than ever before. Comprehensive information about basic biology, preventive medicine, medical and surgical treatments, and related ethical and public policy issues can help you arm yourself with the knowledge you need to be healthy throughout your life.

FOREWORD

Dale C. Garell, M.D.

Advances in our understanding of health and disease during the 20th century have been truly remarkable. Indeed, it could be argued that modern health care is one of the greatest accomplishments in all of human history. In the early 20th century, improvements in sanitation, water treatment, and sewage disposal reduced death rates and increased longevity. Previously untreatable illnesses can now be managed with antibiotics, immunizations, and modern surgical techniques. Discoveries in the fields of immunology, genetic diagnosis, and organ transplantation are revolutionizing the prevention and treatment of disease. Modern medicine is even making inroads against cancer and heart disease, two of the leading causes of death in the United States.

Although there is much to be proud of, medicine continues to face enormous challenges. Science has vanquished diseases such as smallpox and polio, but new killers, most notably AIDS, confront us. Moreover, we now victimize ourselves with what some have called "diseases of choice," or those brought on by drug and alcohol abuse, bad eating habits, and mismanagement of the stresses and strains of contemporary life. The very technology that is doing so much to prolong life has brought with it previously unimaginable ethical dilemmas related to issues of death and dying. The rising cost of health care is a matter of central concern to us all. And violence in the form of automobile accidents, homicide, and suicide remains the major killer of young adults.

In the past, most people were content to leave health care and medical treatment in the hands of professionals. But since the 1960s, the consumer of medical care—that is, the patient—has assumed an increasingly central role in the management of his or her own health. There has also been a new emphasis placed on prevention: People are recognizing that their own actions can help prevent many of the conditions that have caused death and disease in the past. This accounts for the growing commitment to good nutrition and regular exercise, for the increasing number of people who are choosing not to smoke, and for a new moderation in people's drinking habits.

People want to know more about themselves and their own health. They are curious about their body: its anatomy, physiology, and biochemistry. They want to keep up with rapidly evolving medical technologies and procedures. They are willing to educate themselves about common disorders and diseases so that they can be full partners in their own health care.

THE ENCYCLOPEDIA OF HEALTH is designed to provide the basic knowledge that readers will need if they are to take significant responsibility for their own health. It is also meant to serve as a frame of reference for further study and exploration. The encyclopedia is divided into five subsections: The Healthy Body; The Life Cycle; Medical Disorders & Their Treatment; Psychological Disorders & Their Treatment; and Medical Issues. For each topic covered by the encyclopedia, we present the essential facts about the relevant biology; the symptoms, diagnosis, and treatment of common diseases and disorders; and ways in which you can prevent or reduce the severity of health problems when that is possible. The encyclopedia also projects what may lie ahead in the way of future treatment or prevention strategies.

The broad range of topics and issues covered in the encyclopedia reflects that human health encompasses physical, psychological, social, environmental, and spiritual well-being. Just as the mind and the body are inextricably linked, so, too, is the individual an integral part of the wider world that comprises his or her family, society, and environment. To discuss health in its broadest aspect it is necessary to explore the many ways in which it is connected to such fields as law, social science, public policy, economics, and even religion. And so, the encyclopedia is meant to be a bridge between science, medical technology, the world at large, and you. I hope that it will inspire you to pursue in greater depth particular areas of interest and that you will take advantage of the suggestions for further reading and the lists of resources and organizations that can provide additional information.

CHAPTER 1

A WIDESPREAD AND INCURABLE ILLNESS

Actress Gloria Loring and her son, who has diabetes

More than 11 million people in the United States have *diabetes mellitus*. Approximately 1 out of every 20 Americans has the disease. Although significant progress has been made in controlling it, there is still no cure. Diabetes is a serious and lifelong illness. With early detection and treatment, however, diabetics can lead relatively normal lives and dangerous complications can be avoided or delayed.

Diabetes is a disease in which the cells of the body starve to death in the midst of plenty. Sugar, in the form of *glucose*, is the most important source of energy for all living tissue. Whether a person is sound asleep or very active, the cells of the body need a constant supply of this fuel to survive. Most of the glucose that the body needs is provided by foods high in *carbohydrates*. These are foods that contain a large quantity of sugar or starch. Bread, fruit, ice cream, and cereal are good examples of foods that are high in carbohydrates.

As these foods are digested, the carbohydrates are converted into glucose. The glucose is absorbed into the bloodstream and circulates throughout the body. In order to be used, however, the glucose has to gain entry into the cells that need it. *Insulin*, a hormone produced by the *pancreas*, controls this process. Insulin allows glucose to penetrate cell membranes. Once inside the cells, glucose can be used as quick energy or it can be stored for later use. In healthy individuals, the amount of glucose in the blood automatically controls the rate of insulin production in the pancreas. But if not enough insulin is produced, or if the insulin is not used effectively, the cells cannot absorb the glucose. When this happens, the tissues of the body have no fuel to carry on the processes of life, and the unused sugar builds up in the blood. This is diabetes.

The body attempts to deal with this imbalance by filtering out excess glucose through the kidneys, resulting in high levels of sugar in the urine. As glucose levels rise, however, the kidneys are over-whelmed and stop functioning normally. They lose their ability to absorb water effectively, which results in abnormally frequent urination. This is commonly the earliest sign of diabetes. It is often accompanied by unquenchable thirst as the body tries to replenish lost fluids.

Cellular starvation results in weakness, weight loss, and the inability to lead a normal life, but the excess blood sugar itself can also cause immediate and long-term illnesses. It can produce a diabetic *coma*, or period of unconsciousness, and over time it can damage nerves, weaken the circulatory system, impair healing, and endanger pregnancies.

Some people are more likely to develop diabetes than others. In adults over 45 years of age, women are diagnosed with the disease more frequently than men. Heredity also plays a role. In some families the disease is common, whereas in others it appears rarely. Although it is

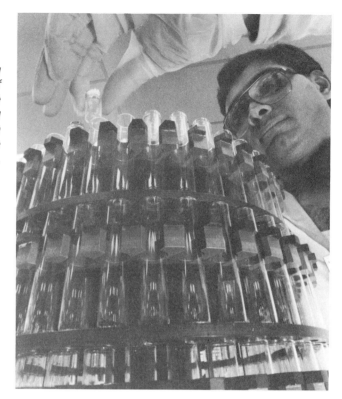

Genetic engineering and the science of molecular biology have raised hopes that a cure for diabetes can be found before the end of the 20th century.

impossible to change a person's sex or his or her family's medical history, there is one risk factor for diabetes that most people can control: obesity. People who are grossly overweight are very likely to become diabetic.

THE HUMAN COST

According to the American Diabetes Association, diabetics spend a total of more than 24 million days in hospitals each year in the United States. Nearly 6,000 people lose their eyesight annually because of diabetes, making it the most common cause of adult blindness. People with diabetes are at least twice as likely to develop heart disease and suffer heart attacks and strokes. They have kidney problems 17 times more frequently than people without diabetes and undergo 40 times as many amputations. Diabetes is the direct cause of more than 40,000 deaths a year and an indirect cause of more than 300,000 deaths a year, counting patients who die of diabetes-related kidney, heart, and circulatory problems. Diabetes is the third most common cause of death in the United States today, after heart disease and cancer.

Although these statistics can be frightening, most people with diabetes are able to live normal lives. This requires keeping blood sugar levels under control. For some diabetics, daily insulin injections are necessary. For most people with diabetes, however, a proper diet and regular exercise are sufficient.

Until medical science can provide a cure for diabetes, people with this disease must take an active role in maintaining good health. In *The Diabetes Fact Book* (Charles Scribner's Sons, 1982), Dr. Theodore G. Duncan quotes Dr. Charles H. Best, one of the researchers who first discovered insulin: "Diabetics who take care of themselves have an excellent chance for a completely normal life." Recognizing the early signs of diabetes is crucial to this goal. Unfortunately, as many as 5 million people in the United States have diabetes and do not know it.

This book will explore the causes of diabetes, how to lower the risk of getting the disease, how it can be controlled, and how people with diabetes can live well and live long.

CHAPTER 2

THE DISCOVERY PROCESS

Doctor Charles H. Best,
codiscoverer of insulin, in 1971

Diabetes is an ancient disease. No one knows exactly how old, but the first written reports appear in an ancient Egyptian manuscript, the Ebers papyrus, dating back to 1500 B.C., which presents a fairly accurate description of the disease. It also mentions the relentless thirst common to diabetics. Early Arabic and Chinese medical records relate another common symptom, frequent and excessive urination. Although the disease was poorly understood, ancient medical practitioners did suspect that high sugar levels were involved. They developed a crude but fairly effective diagnostic test. A sample of a patient's urine was poured on the ground near an anthill. If the urine attracted ants, it was considered proof that sugar was present.

In the 2nd century A.D., the Greek physician Aretaeus named the disease *diabetes*, using the ancient Greek word meaning "to siphon" or "to flow through" because excessive urination was one of the first and most distinctive symptoms of the illness. The ancient Greeks believed that in some fashion the flesh of the body was melting down and being transformed into urine. Somewhat later, Roman physicians added the Latin word *mellitus*, meaning "sweetened" or "honeylike," and today diabetes mellitus remains the formal name of the disease.

DIAGNOSIS AND EARLY TREATMENT

As with many other diseases, unfortunately, it was simply impossible for people of the prescientific age to understand what caused diabetes, let alone develop truly effective treatments. The medieval physician Maimonides, practicing in the 12th century, observed that diabetes was more common in Egypt than in Spain, and he wrongly concluded that people living in hot climates were more likely to get the disease. Paracelsus, the Swiss physician, alchemist, and philosopher, thought by many to be the greatest medical mind of the 16th century, ignored the work of the early Greeks and mistakenly claimed that diabetes was caused by a salt imbalance. Inadequate scientific method held back the growth of useful medical knowledge.

The 17th-century scientist Thomas Willis put diabetes research back on the right track. He proved once and for all that sugar, not salt, identified the disease. Willis's laboratory test was quite simple. He tasted the urine of his diabetic patients and found it to be sweet. In the absence of more effective techniques, the taste test became very common for more than a century. At the beginning of the 18th century, the researcher Matthew Dobson expanded on Willis's method and tasted both the urine and the blood of patients with diabetes. Both bodily fluids were found to be sweet.

At the time, doctors had little to offer their diabetic patients. Many treatments were tried but nothing was very effective. During the siege of Paris at the end of the Franco-Prussian War in 1871, food supplies became very scarce. Doctors observed that diabetic patients who became victims of the famine seemed to gain greater control over the progression of their disease. So the only approach that seemed to prolong life was to drastically reduce the intake of carbohydrates. This seemed to reduce the level of blood sugar, but it required a near-starvation diet. A typical treatment program required that, for a minimum of one day every week, patients not be allowed to eat anything at all. Many patients who resisted this treatment were actually locked up to keep them from eating.

FOCUS ON THE PANCREAS

In 1869, Paul Langerhans, a German medical student, made microscopic examinations of tissue samples from the pancreas. He observed tiny groups of cells throughout the pancreas that appeared to clump together. These clusters of cells were later named the *islets of Langerhans* in honor of his discovery, but at the time he identified them no one had yet isolated the hormone insulin or even guessed at the role of these cells in producing it.

The relationship between diabetes and the pancreas was proved in 1889 by Oskar Minkowski and Joseph von Mering. These two researchers met at the University of Strasbourg in France, where Minkowski had been assisting Bernard Naunyn, the world's leading expert in diabetes. Von Mering had joined the faculty of the Department of Physiological Chemistry.

Minkowski and von Mering's discovery, like so many others, was a result of ignorance of what the so-called experts had already decided; it was also an opportune interpretation of unexpected experimental results. At the time they met, von Mering was studying how the body absorbed fat. He believed that if the pancreas was not working properly, some fat was being poorly utilized. Von Mering attempted to test his hypothesis by operating on a dog and tying off all of the ducts leading from its pancreas. No matter how hard he tried, pancreatic secretions still managed to leak out. Minkowski, a rather accomplished experimental surgeon, offered to remove the dog's entire pancreas.

At the time, neither doctor anticipated that what they were doing had anything to do with diabetes. Nor were they aware that far more prominent men of science had ruled out any relationship between the pancreas and diabetes. Von Mering delivered the dog and Minkowski performed the surgery. While the dog was recovering from surgery, von Mering had to rush out of town unexpectedly. While he was gone, the dog was allowed to run free in the laboratory. It was already housebroken, and von Mering's assistant was supposed to train it to urinate and defecate at specific times and at a specific location.

When Minkowski visited the lab, he found that the dog was urinating all over the place, and he complained to von Mering's lab assistant. Their conversation was reported in Minkowski's article, "Historical Development of the Theory of Pancreatic Diabetes," reprinted in the January 1989 issue of *Diabetes*. The lab assistant told Minkowski, "I did train him, but this animal is quite peculiar. No sooner does he empty his bladder completely when he has to urinate again and again." Curious, Minkowski collected some of the dog's urine and tested it for glucose. The level was excessively high. When von Mering

Oskar Minkowski, who along with Joseph von Mering in 1889 conducted the experiment proving that diabetes was related to a failure of the pancreas

Dr. Frederick Banting and student Charles H. Best, codiscoverers of insulin, with one of the first diabetic dogs to have its life prolonged by insulin

returned, they repeated the experiment on several other dogs. The same result was achieved each time. Minkowski and von Mering realized that they had stumbled upon an important discovery: For the first time, there was proof that diabetes was related to disturbances of the pancreas.

Other researchers now began to focus their attention on the pancreas. In 1902, Eugene L. Opie discovered tissue degeneration in the islets of Langerhans when he autopsied the bodies of diabetics. Others carefully studied the cellular structure of the pancreas and its various secretions, until it was strongly suspected that some hormone produced by the gland had a role to play in the absorption of sugar by the body.

INSULIN—A GIANT STEP FORWARD

The great breakthrough came in 1921, with the discovery of insulin. Dr. Frederick Banting, a Canadian doctor who specialized in orthopedic surgery, and Charles Best, a young medical student, set out to isolate a substance from the pancreas that could be used to lower blood sugar. For an entire summer, they experimented with extracts of pancreatic tissue. Finally, they identified a substance from the islets of Langerhans. They called this substance *isletin*, which was later changed to insulin. Banting and Best injected isletin extracted from a normal dog's pancreas into a dog diagnosed with diabetes. Almost immediately, the diabetic dog's blood sugar level dropped. Repeating this experiment several times convinced them that they had truly discovered what they had set out to find.

Shortly after, an 11-year-old boy named Leonard Thompson became the first human subject to receive insulin injections for his diabetes. Leonard, who had been kept alive on a starvation diet, was extremely weak and could barely get out of bed. With nothing to lose, his parents agreed to allow Dr. Banting to administer insulin. The results were amazing. Once insulin therapy began, Leonard was able to eat a nearly normal diet. He gained weight and strength and became an active child. In 1923, Banting and Best were awarded a Nobel Prize for their discovery of insulin.

Unfortunately, insulin does not actually cure diabetes. Before its discovery, however, diabetics who could not produce insulin had a life expectancy that could be measured in weeks or months. With the availability of insulin therapy, most of these people could now expect to live a nearly normal life.

CHAPTER 3

THE DYNAMICS OF INSULIN

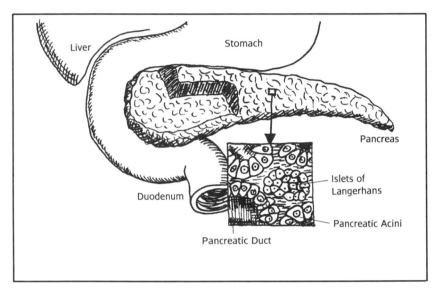

The pancreas

In your abdomen, just below and behind your stomach, is a long, narrow organ known as the pancreas. It is approximately six inches in length and weighs less than half a pound. The pancreas is both an *exocrine* and an *endocrine* gland. Exocrine glands secrete their products through ducts or channels to a specific location. In contrast, endocrine glands release their secretions directly into the bloodstream. As an exocrine gland, the pancreas produces digestive enzymes that flow through ducts to the small intestine, where they help to chemically break down the food we eat into digestible substances. As an endocrine gland, the pancreas produces hormones that travel freely throughout the body in the blood, acting as chemical regulators of different types of cellular activity.

Most of the gland is used for the production of digestive enzymes. The production of hormones is restricted to the islets of Langerhans. There are a half million to a million of these islets, and yet these tiny clusters of cells make up less than 2% of the entire pancreas.

Three distinct types of cells have been identified within the islets: *alpha cells*, *beta cells*, and *delta cells*. The beta cells, numbering between 1,000 and 2,000 per islet, are the most numerous and the most important. These cells manufacture, store, and release insulin. Normally, the level of insulin production is determined by the amount of glucose circulating in the blood. The beta cells constantly measure the level of glucose and pump out just enough insulin to deal with it.

The alpha cells produce a hormone called *glucagon*. If blood sugar levels fall too low, glucagon will be released. This hormone increases blood sugar levels by converting sugar stored in the liver into glucose. The two hormones, insulin and glucagon, work in tandem to make sure that enough sugar is available in the bloodstream and that the cells of the body can extract the sugar from the blood as they need it.

The delta cells manufacture the hormone known as *somatostatin*. Researchers are uncertain as to its exact function, though it is thought to play some role in regulating the balance between insulin and glucagon.

FUELING THE BODY

As we digest our food, it is broken down into six key elements: water, minerals, vitamins, carbohydrates, proteins, and fats. Of these, only carbohydrates, proteins, and fats can be used as fuel by the body, and all are affected by insulin.

Carbohydrates are found in almost every food that we eat. Foods high in sugar or starch are particularly good sources of carbohydrates.

As we digest these foods, the carbohydrates are broken down into glucose. Glucose is a very simple sugar. It easily and rapidly passes into the bloodstream. It is the greatest and the quickest source of energy of all possible fuels.

Once in the bloodstream, glucose travels throughout the body. As it passes through the pancreas, it stimulates receptors on the surface of the beta cells that respond only to sugar-shaped molecules. The receptors act like prongs. They capture the sugar molecules and send a signal to the interior of the beta cell. As the concentration of glucose rises, the number of receptors stimulated by sugar molecules increases and the signal gets stronger. The amount of insulin released by the beta cells is regulated by the strength of this signal. Eating an orange will ring some bells, but a hot fudge sundae is a "four-alarmer."

Within the beta cells are microscopic chambers called *secretory granules*. Here, insulin is stored and released whenever the body must react quickly to a sudden increase in blood sugar. This is likely to occur immediately following a meal or a sweet snack. If the level of sugar remains high, sugar molecules will continue to stimulate the receptors, and the beta cells will produce additional insulin, so that for most nondiabetic people, it is almost impossible for blood sugar levels to reach dangerously high levels, no matter what they eat.

One of the myths about diabetes is that it can be triggered by eating too many sweets. This is nearly impossible. An individual may get cavities, and he or she may gain weight, but unless a sweet tooth causes a person to become grossly overweight, the normal insulin response should be able to deal with any level of excess sugar.

INSULIN AT WORK

Insulin allows cells to absorb and use glucose. Once secreted, insulin molecules circulate freely in the bloodstream until they attach to insulin receptors on the outer membranes of cells. Once attached, insulin plays a crucial role as a gatekeeper. It attracts glucose and directs it through the protective membrane to the cell's interior. Here, the glucose is used for instant energy or stored for later use.

As glucose is absorbed, some is used immediately, while some is converted into *glycogen* and stored in the liver and muscles until needed. Glycogen can quickly be changed back into glucose with the help of glucagon, the hormone secreted by the alpha cells of the pancreas. Running coaches are well aware of the value of glycogen and often instruct their athletes to eat a big pasta dinner before an important race. The high-carbohydrate meal helps to boost supplies of glycogen. Although instant energy and adrenaline will get a runner off the starting block, reserve energy may determine how well he or she finishes the race. Glucose that is not used as quick energy or stored as glycogen is converted by the liver into fat and stored in fat cells throughout the body.

PROTEIN AND FAT

Protein is found in a wide variety of foods. Some of the most common sources are milk, fish, cheese, grains, nuts, meat, and eggs. As it is digested, protein is broken down into *amino acids*. These are the building blocks that our body uses to create new tissue or repair damaged tissue. Both of these processes require insulin. If it is not available, wounds will not heal properly. Small children who do not produce enough insulin frequently do not grow at a normal rate.

Protein is also an important secondary source of glucose. If the supply from carbohydrates is insufficient, amino acids can be turned into glucose. Insulin is used in this process as well as in the conversion of excess amino acids into fat.

Although few people have anything good to say about fat, reasonable amounts are crucial to maintaining good health. Fat serves as a reserve source of energy and plays an important role in delivering vitamins A, D, E, and K to the bloodstream. Many of the foods rich in protein, such as cheese, milk, and beef, are also high in fat. Of everything we consume, fat takes the longest to digest, and it has twice as many calories as protein or carbohydrates. Most of the fat in our body is composed of *triglycerides*, a compound made from three fatty acids. Insulin allows the triglycerides to leave the bloodstream and enter fat cells, where they are stored. It also keeps triglycerides from breaking down.

WHEN DISASTER STRIKES

A constant supply of glucose is crucial to keep our body functioning smoothly. Although all organs need glucose, the brain is the most demanding consumer. It wants glucose, and it wants it continually. Although the muscles, the heart, and other organs can thrive on a mixture of fuels, the brain does not accept substitutes. When glucose levels fall below normal, the brain broadcasts its dissatisfaction. Confusion, poor concentration, and light-headedness are some of the earliest symptoms. When an individual is too busy to stop and eat and waits too long, he or she probably will notice a lessened ability to think clearly. This is a mild warning that the brain is starving. People who

Rosalyn Yalow receives the Nobel Prize from King Carl Gustaf of Sweden. Dr. Yalow, along with Dr. Saul Berson, developed a test to measure amounts of insulin in the bloodstream, enabling physicians to distinguish between the two types of diabetes.

experiment with fad diets often feel faint and confused long before they experience any loss of weight.

If insulin is not available, glucose cannot get into the cells of the brain or any other organ. Without insulin, the level of circulating glucose rises higher and higher. This causes *hyperglycemia*, a condition characterized by abnormally high blood sugar.

Without glucose, the cells begin to starve. They issue increasingly urgent demands for fuel. The body literally begins to cannibalize itself, breaking down amino acids and fat to meet its voracious, relentless appetite. Unfortunately, these sources of energy are far less efficient than glucose. In converting fat to energy, acidic compounds known as *ketones* are produced as a by-product. Normally, our need for fuel drawn from fat is low enough to keep the level of ketones safely in check. When glucose is not available to our cells, however, protein and fat are rapidly converted and ketones flood the blood and urine. At extreme levels, a condition known as *ketoacidosis* results. Acidic toxins are produced faster than they can be eliminated and the body is poisoned by them. This can lead to decreased appetite, nausea, vomiting, and even death. Diabetes is the most common cause of hyperglycemia and ketoacidosis.

CLARIFYING THE DIAGNOSIS

Until relatively recently, medical experts assumed that all diabetes resulted from a lack of insulin. This proved to be true only in a small percentage of cases. Most diabetics produce insulin; their bodies just cannot use it properly.

In 1950, Dr. Saul Berson and Dr. Rosalyn Yalow, researchers working together in New York City, developed the first procedure to detect and measure insulin in the bloodstream by first making the insulin molecules radioactive. When the test was given to a group of diabetics, Berson and Yalow found that although some diabetics had little or no measurable insulin, many others showed normal amounts of the hormone. In fact, overweight adult diabetics tended to have greater than normal amounts of insulin in their blood. Berson and

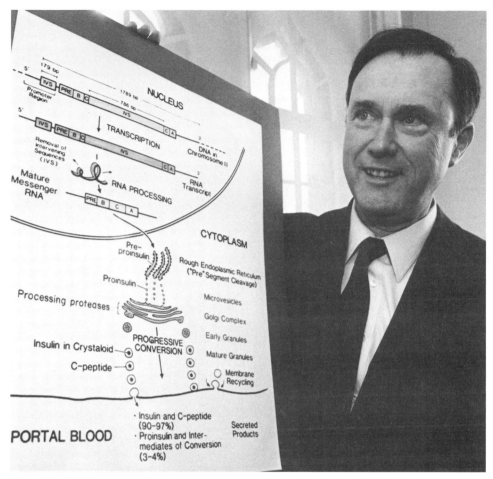

Professor Donald F. Steiner, one of many contemporary researchers who have used the tools of molecular biology to determine how the pancreas manufactures insulin

Yalow's discovery forced doctors to recognize that there was more than one cause of diabetes. Although lack of insulin was confirmed as a cause, it was no longer the only possible cause. Though the exact mechanism is still not understood, many people are hyperglycemic because they cannot effectively use the insulin their bodies produce. This knowledge changed the diagnosis and treatment of diabetes forever. Now, doctors classify their diabetic patients as either *Type I*, those who cannot produce sufficient insulin, or *Type II*, those who produce insulin but are unable to use it properly.

The following chapters will explore the similarities and differences between Type I and Type II diabetes in greater detail.

CHAPTER 4

TYPE I DIABETES

Type I diabetics must regularly test their blood sugar level

Type I diabetes is that form of diabetes caused by the insufficient production of insulin. Another name that frequently appears in medical literature is *insulin-dependent diabetes mellitus*, or IDDM. This name is used because everyone with this form of diabetes must be treated with insulin every day. In the past, this disease was also known as *juvenile diabetes* or *juvenile-onset diabetes*. Most, although not all, people with Type I diabetes are diagnosed when they are children or young adults. The disease can occur at any age, however, so the term *juvenile diabetes* is not really accurate.

THE PANCREAS AS BATTLEGROUND

According to the National Institute of Diabetes and Digestive and Kidney Diseases, 10% of all diabetics have Type I diabetes. Approximately 1 out of every 600 children in the United States has the disease. Type I diabetes is caused by the destruction of the beta cells in the pancreas, the body's only natural source of insulin. For years, scientists recognized that some agent was capable of infiltrating the pancreas, searching out the islets of Langerhans, and killing these cells. The resulting destruction is called *insulitis*.

At first, researchers believed that a virus was the enemy. This hypothesis was supported because abnormally large numbers of *macrophages*, *lymphocytes*, and *antibodies* could be found in the pancreatic islets of people with Type I diabetes. Macrophages and lymphocytes are cells that attack and digest foreign elements in the body such as bacteria or viruses. Antibodies are complex molecules that perform the same function. All are part of the *immune system*, which is designed to distinguish the body's own cells from these dangerous invaders. When foreign cells are detected, battalions of killer cells and killer chemicals are released by the immune system to wipe out the enemy. The strong immune system response seemed to indicate the presence of a disease organism, and indeed there is evidence that in some cases diabetes appears after an attack of mumps, chicken pox, measles, influenza, or some other childhood viral infection.

Unfortunately, this line of research has proved inconclusive, and scientists know that sometimes the immune system makes mistakes. It can even launch an attack on normal cells not infected with a disease organism. This is known as an *autoimmune reaction*. It is now believed that this is the leading cause of insulitis. The immune system of people with Type I diabetes reacts to their own islets' cells as though they were foreign bodies. Killer cells are rushed into the pancreas, rapidly and

Studies of identical twins have revealed that heredity is an important factor in determining who will suffer from diabetes, but it is not the sole deciding factor.

efficiently destroying the beta cells. The islets then lose their ability to produce insulin.

A slightly different theory postulates that Type I diabetes is the result of both a viral invasion and an autoimmune reaction. Advocates of this theory believe that the virus enters the body and infiltrates the beta cells. In attempting to kill the virus, the immune system attacks all of the cells that are hosting the enemy invaders. Unfortunately, these happen to be the beta cells. Further research is necessary to determine whether the body's killer cells are attacking the beta cells because they mistake them for foreign cells or if the attack is in response to a real viral infection. The end result, however, is the same: Type I diabetes.

Heredity also plays a role in the development of Type I diabetes. In studying identical twins, researchers have found that if one twin gets Type I diabetes, his or her twin has approximately a 50% chance of getting it as well. The importance of heredity, however, is not fully understood. It also appears to be a less significant factor for Type I diabetes than for Type II, discussed in the next chapter. People with Type I diabetes report fewer relatives with the disease than do people with Type II.

DIAGNOSING DIABETES

The onset of Type I diabetes is sudden. Symptoms develop usually in a matter of weeks or sometimes in just a few days. Excessive urination and extreme thirst are common reactions, as are stomach pains, vomiting, fatigue, and blurred vision. In small children, bed-wetting can become a sudden problem. As cells begin to starve, the body tries to compensate by converting stored fat into fuel, resulting in a rapid loss of weight, constant hunger, and the release of ketones, acid by-products of the breakdown of fat that give the breath a fruity odor. In large amounts, ketones act like a poison, upsetting delicate chemical balances in the blood, a condition known as ketoacidosis. If untreated, this can lead to diabetic coma, or diabetes-related unconsciousness. Unfortunately, passing out and waking up in the hospital is often a young person's first experience with the disease, and it can be frightening.

If diabetes is suspected, a variety of laboratory tests will be ordered to confirm the diagnosis. Excess ketones can be detected in the urine. Excess sugar will also show up in urine samples, but urine sugar tests are not reliable. Some people have kidneys with a very low threshold for sugar. Glucose will appear in their urine even though their blood sugar levels are normal. In some cases, blood glucose levels can be abnormally high while urine sugar tests will be negative. It may take hours or days until high blood sugar results in glucose in the urine. For people who are known diabetics, however, urine tests are helpful in the routine monitoring of glucose levels.

The first and simplest of the tests used to detect diabetes is known as the *fasting blood sugar test*, performed after a person has had nothing to eat or drink except water for at least 10 hours. A small blood sample is taken and the glucose level is analyzed. If high levels of glucose are detected, it is a good indication of diabetes. But if excess sugar is not present, further tests are still called for. A *postprandial test* measures glucose levels after a meal high in carbohydrates. Blood sugar is usually at its highest level 30 to 60 minutes after eating. If maximum levels exceed normal, diabetes may be the cause. For an initial diagnosis, however, it may be difficult to know what is a normal glucose level for a particular individual.

For this reason, and because errors sometimes occur in laboratory tests, most doctors will not confirm a diagnosis of diabetes without a *glucose tolerance test*. The night before the test, the patient is told not to eat anything after 10:00 P.M. The following morning, a sample of blood is taken and analyzed to determine the amount of sugar it contains. Blood sugar levels should be low at this point, and this first blood sample provides a baseline for comparison with later measurements.

The patient is then given an extremely sweet, high-glucose solution to drink. The patient's blood is drawn again one hour, two hours, and three hours later. The doctor can then observe how fast and how effectively the body responds. With nondiabetics, blood sugar levels will return to the baseline level within three hours. If the sugar level is still high several hours after the test begins, it is a strong indication that glucose is not being absorbed properly.

INSULIN THERAPY

The only effective treatment for Type I diabetes is insulin therapy. Insulin was first commercially manufactured in the United States in 1923, two years after Banting and Best isolated and tested the hormone. The earliest supplies of insulin were inconsistent in strength and contained many impurities, and up until recently they were taken from the pancreas of pigs and cows. Of all the common animal species, pigs and cows produce insulin that is most similar to human insulin. Although most diabetics tolerate this insulin well, some people experience allergic reactions. Scientists can now chemically transform insulin from pigs into insulin that is identical to the form produced by humans. Recent advances have also resulted in better quality control. Now, insulin derived from cows and pigs is 99% pure.

The pancreas is a relatively small organ, and it takes approximately 10,000 pounds of pancreas to make just 1 pound of insulin. An enormous number of animals would be needed to supply diabetics around the world with enough insulin. Fortunately, a major breakthrough occurred in 1978. Genentech, a biotechnology company in California, developed a process that produces human insulin through genetic engineering.

Using Genentech's technology, the deoxyribonucleic acid (DNA) that controls the production of human insulin is isolated and then spliced into the genetic material of rapidly growing bacteria. The bacteria multiply quickly and generate human insulin in large amounts. In the final step, the insulin is separated from the bacteria. Insulin was the first product made using recombinant DNA technology to be approved by the Food and Drug Administration. Using this technology, the Eli Lilly Company has become the largest insulin manufacturer in the United States. For the first time ever, unlimited supplies of human insulin are readily available.

Whether it is derived from animals or genetically engineered bacteria, virtually all of the insulin produced since the 1980s is highly purified and concentrated, reducing the quantity of fluid that has to be injected. Needles have become smaller and injections are now relatively painless. Earlier forms of insulin lasted only six to eight hours, which meant that most Type I diabetics needed three to four shots every day. By adding chemicals such as protamine and zinc, scientists are now able to alter how quickly the insulin begins to work, when insulin action will peak, and how long the insulin will be effective.

The original insulin formula is now known as short-acting insulin. Like the hormone produced naturally in the bodies of nondiabetics, it begins transporting glucose across cell membranes in less than half an hour after injection and reaches peak activity in two to four hours. Two new forms of insulin are now available. *Lente*, also known as NPH or intermediate-acting insulin, is a little slower. It begins to work 2 hours after injection, peaks after 8 to 12 hours, and lasts for 24 hours. *Ultralente*, or long-acting insulin, works for nearly a day and a half.

Having a variety of insulin formulas allows doctors to provide diabetic patients with a customized regimen of insulin therapy, mini-

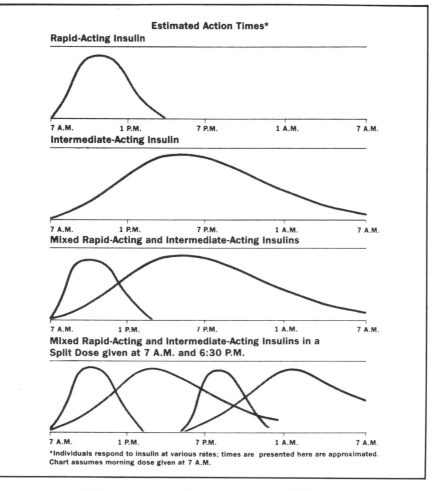

Estimated Action Times*

Rapid-Acting Insulin

7 A.M. 1 P.M. 7 P.M. 1 A.M. 7 A.M.

Intermediate-Acting Insulin

7 A.M. 1 P.M. 7 P.M. 1 A.M. 7 A.M.

Mixed Rapid-Acting and Intermediate-Acting Insulins

7 A.M. 1 P.M. 7 P.M. 1 A.M. 7 A.M.

Mixed Rapid-Acting and Intermediate-Acting Insulins in a Split Dose given at 7 A.M. and 6:30 P.M.

7 A.M. 1 P.M. 7 P.M. 1 A.M. 7 A.M.

*Individuals respond to insulin at various rates; times are presented here are approximated. Chart assumes morning dose given at 7 A.M.

The American Diabetes Association has prepared this chart to assist insulin-dependent diabetics in quickly determining whether they are experiencing a reaction to an overdose of insulin (hypoglycemia) or an excess of sugar in their blood (hyperglycemia or ketoacidosis).

mizing the number of injections. It also makes it easier to adjust treatment for young children, whose needs continue to change as they grow.

Unfortunately, doctors have not been able to eliminate the need for insulin injections. Insulin cannot be given orally. Enzymes of the digestive system destroy the hormone before it can enter the bloodstream.

Injecting Insulin

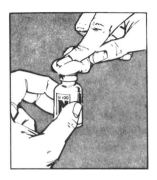

The insulin bottle
is sterilized

The syringe is filled
with air

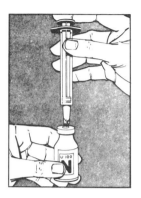

Air is injected into
the insulin bottle

Insulin is injected *subcutaneously*, that is, into the fatty tissue under the skin, rather than *intravenously*, or directly into the bloodstream through a vein. This technique permits a slower and more even rate of absorption into the blood and is also simpler and less painful for people without medical training.

Diabetics must also learn the technique of *site rotation*. To avoid swellings, bumps, puffiness, and other skin irritations caused by continually injecting the same area, diabetics develop various systems for changing injection sites daily. One day it may be the back of the upper arm; the next day the fatty area of the thigh; the third day the buttocks. Within these general locations the diabetic may choose a different injection site, using, for example, four different spots on the thigh before moving on to the arm.

Both the top of the insulin bottle and the skin at the injection site are disinfected with a cotton swab soaked in alcohol. Longer-acting insulin bottles are gently rolled between the palms of the hands to evenly mix the suspension. The plunger of the syringe is pulled out to the required number of units and the syringe is allowed to fill with air.

The needle is pushed into the skin

The syringe is filled with insulin

With the insulin bottle upright, the needle is pushed down into the bottle and the plunger is depressed, pushing air into the insulin. Then the bottle with the syringe still inside is turned upside down. The plunger is slowly pulled back until the syringe fills with slightly more than the required dose of insulin. First injecting air into the bottle and then turning it upside down makes it easier to draw out the insulin. Both air pressure and gravity are working to fill the syringe.

With the needle still inside the insulin bottle, the syringe is gently tapped to force air bubbles up to the top. The plunger is then pushed in slightly to force the air bubbles back into the bottle. The syringe is removed from the bottle, and the diabetic checks once more to see if the correct number of units has been drawn.

At the injection site, the skin is grasped, pinched, and pulled up between the thumb and forefinger. The diabetic can feel if he or she has found an area of fatty tissue or has accidentally grasped muscle tissue. The syringe is held by the barrel and pushed straight down into the skin, and the plunger is pushed down with a gentle, even pressure.

With the needles in use today and the subcutaneous injection technique, insulin shots are relatively painless. Occasionally the needle will hit a small blood vessel. The bleeding is not serious, and with refined techniques the diabetic can easily learn to avoid injecting insulin directly into his or her blood.

CONTROLLING DIABETES

The overall goal in controlling diabetes is to maintain the efficient metabolism of food. However, even with all the advances in insulin therapy, controlling Type I diabetes requires a considerable commitment and effort. Perhaps no other disease requires so much personal involvement. Diabetics and their families work with a whole team of professionals—doctors, nurses, nutritionists, and dietitians—whose goal is to help the person achieve control over his or her diabetes, to assist in monitoring the disease, and to provide guidance as the person grows older or as his or her life-style changes.

For insulin therapy to be effective, a sensible meal plan must be developed. By reducing the intake of foods high in fat or sugar, people with Type I diabetes can decrease the amount of insulin they will need. By eating meals and snacks at approximately the same time each day, diabetics can maximize the benefits of insulin and minimize the risks associated with poor timing. It is important to have plenty of glucose in the body when insulin activity is at its strongest.

Regular exercise also offers benefits for people with diabetes. Exercise can lower blood glucose levels, improve circulation, and help the body to use glucose. For diabetics, exercise should be a part of their normal routine. Before undertaking an exercise program, however, diabetics should talk to their doctors. As activity levels increase, so does the need for fuel.

MONITORING VITAL BODY FLUIDS

Daily testing of blood and urine allows people with Type I diabetes to evaluate how well their treatment plan is working. Regular testing and record keeping provide valuable information for monitoring and adjusting insulin schedules as well as providing an early warning if dangerous imbalances occur.

Most people with Type I diabetes check their glucose level several times a day. Usually this is done before meals and before bed. It is accomplished with one of a number of blood-test kits that are so simple even young children can be taught to use them. Using a special needle, a tiny, nearly painless prick is made in a fingertip and one drop of blood is placed onto a special chemically treated paper test strip. The amount of glucose in the blood will change the color of the strip. The color of the strip is compared to a chart on the package, or the strip is inserted into a device that reads out the results. The test can be done almost anywhere and takes just a minute or two. It is important, however, that results be recorded every day so that measurements can be compared over a long period of time.

Although urine tests are not very effective for measuring blood sugar, they offer important information about the production of ketones. Our body can tolerate only very low levels of ketones. It is the kidneys' job to remove these poisons from the circulatory system. Daily urine tests will provide advance warning if ketone levels are rising. Most Type I diabetics perform this test every morning. Again, a test strip is dabbed in a urine sample, and the resulting color of the strip is compared to a color chart on the package. This test indicates whether the ketones are at a low, moderate, or dangerous level.

SUDDEN COMPLICATIONS

Improved insulin products and daily testing have greatly decreased the frequency of medical emergencies caused by Type I diabetes. These advances, however, cannot entirely eliminate the possibility of sudden complications. Experiencing stress, skipping a meal, getting a virus, or participating in strenuous activity are just a few of the events that can seriously upset blood sugar levels. For people with a healthy insulin response, the body automatically adjusts. For people with Type I diabetes, a crisis situation may result. If early warning signs are ignored and appropriate action is delayed, the situation may rapidly become life threatening.

The most common sudden complication of Type I diabetes is *hypoglycemia*, an abnormally low blood sugar level. This condition is also known as *insulin reaction* or *insulin shock*. It frequently occurs just before mealtime, especially if scheduling has been thrown off and a meal is delayed. Hypoglycemia may also result from too much

HYPOGLYCEMIC REACTION (Insulin Reaction)	WARNING SIGNS	KETOACIDOSIS (Diabetic Coma)
Sudden	**ONSET**	Gradual
Pale, moist	**SKIN**	Flushed, dry
Excited, nervous, irritable, confused	**BEHAVIOR**	Drowsy
Normal	**BREATH**	Fruity odor (acetone)
Normal to rapid shallow	**BREATHING**	Deep, labored
Absent	**VOMITING**	Present
Moist, numb, tingling	**TONGUE**	Dry
Present	**HUNGER**	Absent
Absent	**THIRST**	Present
Headache	**PAIN**	Abdominal
Absent or slight	**SUGAR IN URINE**	Large amounts

Ketones - chemicals normally produced in the liver from incomplete burning of acids derived from fats and proteins. In uncontrolled diabetes the concentration of ketones becomes very high with a strong acid effect which is called ketoacidosis.

Today, diabetics have a choice of insulin types that maintain their effectiveness over different periods of time. Mixing insulin types can reduce the need for frequent injections.

insulin, not enough food, or an increase in physical activity. Although many diabetics can become hypoglycemic without realizing it, common symptoms include feeling sweaty, shaky, dizzy, or nervous. Blurred vision and headaches are also common. Often, relatives and friends of diabetics recognize the symptoms before the diabetic. A frequent tip-off occurs when the diabetic suddenly exhibits behavior that is totally out of character. In some cases a calm, considerate person will become arrogant and resentful, or a happy, active person may suddenly become withdrawn and quiet.

Because hypoglycemia can interfere with clear thinking, early warning signs may be ignored by the diabetic. Researchers have tested this phenomenon using the "drunkometer," a machine developed by Delco Electronics. Although the drunkometer was designed to measure mental impairment following the consumption of alcohol, it works equally well in evaluating the effects of hypoglycemia. Fifty percent of the diabetics tested whose hypoglycemia was severe enough to make them hazardous drivers were totally unaware that their abilities were impaired. It is important that diabetics let the people close to them know about their condition. Often family members, roommates, and friends are in a much better position than the diabetic to observe early signs of hypoglycemia.

If recognized in time, acute hypoglycemia can easily be treated with any quick source of sugar. A small box of raisins, half a cup of fruit juice, or a candy bar will correct the imbalance.

If untreated, hypoglycemia can cause convulsions or loss of consciousness. At this point, it is dangerous to try to give the person something to eat or drink. The diabetic will need a shot of glucagon, the hormone that instantly converts stored sugar into glucose. Unless there is someone available with glucagon who is experienced in administering it, a diabetic suffering severe hypoglycemia should immediately be taken to a hospital.

DIABETIC COMA

Hyperglycemia, the presence of too much blood sugar, is equally dangerous. Initial symptoms are fatigue, hunger, thirst, excessive urination, and blurred vision. If untreated, hyperglycemia can lead to ketoacidosis or diabetic coma. Blood and urine become permeated with toxic waste products. Even the breath takes on a strange acidic odor. Unfortunately, this can easily be mistaken for alcohol intoxication, and bystanders may believe that the diabetic is drunk rather than in need of immediate medical attention.

Before the discovery of insulin, ketoacidosis frequently resulted in loss of consciousness, coma, and death. In fact, diabetic coma was for a long time the most common cause of death among diabetics. Fortunately, this complication is increasingly rare. Daily urine and blood testing can provide warnings of approaching hyperglycemia and ketoacidosis long before serious symptoms occur. For Type I diabetics, additional insulin or a revised schedule of insulin administration will effectively reverse hyperglycemia.

Although acute complications of Type I diabetes cannot be eliminated, the key to controlling their frequency and severity lies in prevention and early detection. This depends on monitoring blood and urine to make sure that glucose is at normal levels and that ketones are not building up.

CHAPTER 5

TYPE II DIABETES

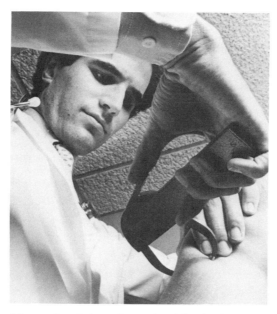

Measuring fat, an important factor in the occurrence of Type II diabetes

Type II diabetes occurs far more frequently than Type I. Approximately 10 million people in the United States have this form of the disease. Because Type II diabetes generally affects people who are 40 or older, it has been called *adult-onset diabetes*. Exceptions do exist, however, and there are documented cases of Type II diabetes occurring in people under 20 years of age. Type II is also identified as *non-insulin-dependent diabetes mellitus*, or NIDDM. Unlike Type I diabetics, most people with Type II do not require daily insulin injections to control their disease. Their beta cells do pump out insulin. Although some Type II diabetics have insulin levels that would be considered low, most have levels that are normal or even higher than normal. What these people all share is an inability to use insulin effectively.

Researchers still have much to learn about the dynamics of Type II diabetes. They do not fully understand where the breakdown occurs. For blood sugar to enter a cell, an insulin molecule must first attach itself to receptors on the cell's outer membrane. Once in place, the insulin allows glucose to be transported across the membrane and into the interior of the cell. Problems can arise at any stage. Insulin receptors may not function properly or may be missing completely. The insulin molecule itself may be chemically malformed and incapable of attracting or transporting glucose into the cell. These problems are usually lumped together under the category of *insulin resistance*, and this is thought to be the underlying cause of Type II diabetes.

Scientists first thought that Type II diabetes might be caused by agents similar to those thought to cause Type I. They investigated the possibility of an autoimmune reaction or a viral invasion. No real evidence could be found, however, to indicate that the beta cells were under attack. Currently, scientists are investigating the possibility that some abnormal cellular chemical product is causing problems or that a normal chemical is being produced in abnormally large amounts.

Recent research indicates that the culprit may be a protein that is secreted along with insulin in the beta cells. This protein, known as *islet-amyloid polypeptide* (IAPP), has been shown to play an important role in the uptake of glucose. Too much IAPP can cause insulin resistance. Some scientists also believe that if IAPP secretion is too high for too long, it can actually create deposits within the beta cells that block the normal production and release of insulin.

TYPE II: RISK FACTORS

Although researchers do not know for sure what causes Type II diabetes, three significant risk factors have been identified. These are heredity, obesity, and age. Of the three, heredity seems to play the most important role. A person's chances of developing Type II diabetes are higher if there is someone else in his or her family who has the disease. It is higher still if there are numerous family members who have diabetes, or if the disease affects relatives on both the mother's and the father's side. A high incidence of Type II diabetes among relatives indicates a genetic link.

If one parent has Type II diabetes, each child will have about a 25% chance of getting it. If both parents have the disease, the risk to each child may be as high as 75%. In identical twins, if one twin gets Type II diabetes, the other twin will get the disease 93% of the time. Many people, however, who come from families where diabetes is common never get the disease. And it is possible for two Type II diabetics to have children who will never be affected. Although heredity is a very important factor, it is not an absolute one.

Age also increases the chances of developing Type II diabetes. As people grow older, their bodies begin to slow down. Tissues process chemicals more slowly and less effectively. Although insulin is available, the body is unable to take full advantage of it, and glucose levels begin to rise dangerously. Most Type II diabetics are diagnosed after the age of 40. In the United States, 20% of everyone over the age of 65 has Type II diabetes, while 25% of the population over 85 is thought to have the disease. As the life span of Americans increases, the number of people with Type II diabetes will continue to increase. According to experts at the International Diabetes Center in Minnesota, more than 15 million Americans over the age of 40 will have Type II diabetes by the year 2000 unless a cure is discovered.

There is little one can do to control one's ancestry or age. A person can exercise quite a bit of control, however, over obesity, the third crucial factor in setting the odds in favor of diabetes. Most people with Type II diabetes are overweight, and many are grossly overweight. Excess fat interferes with the work of insulin. Insulin receptors become less sensitive to the hormone's presence. The receptors also become defective and no longer securely bind insulin molecules to the exterior cell walls. Without a secure binding, the insulin cannot effectively draw glucose from the bloodstream and transmit it to the cell's interior. Glucose levels remain high, which triggers the beta cells to produce even more insulin.

When too much insulin is in the bloodstream, it becomes much more difficult for the body to convert the stored energy of fat into fuel.

Glucose, the most readily available source of energy, cannot be used because it cannot get into the cells that need it. The high glucose level in the blood stimulates abnormally high insulin production. High insulin levels tend to add more fat molecules to the fat cells for storage and to keep stored fat from getting out. So, although an enormous amount of fuel exists, it cannot get into the cells that need it or out of the cells storing it. The body cannot meet its need for fuel. When this happens, people feel hungry all of the time. They cannot control their appetite. The more they eat, the fatter they get. Insulin receptors become even less effective and the imbalance gets worse and worse.

OTHER RISK FACTORS

Sex and race also influence the probability of getting Type II diabetes. Until the age of 30, men have just as great a chance of getting the disease as do women. Beyond 30, however, women make up a larger and larger proportion of the people with this disease. For people 45 and over, women are twice as likely to get the disease as men are.

The incidence of diabetes also varies among racial and ethnic groups. Some American Indian tribes have a much higher rate of Type II diabetes than the general population. It is also known that black Americans are nearly twice as likely to die from diabetes as are white Americans. There has been much debate about this. Some researchers feel the higher incidence of diabetes among blacks is due more to economic and obesity factors than to race. Unfortunately, many black people still occupy lower income groups, and poor people tend to eat poorer-quality food, with a higher fat content. They also do not receive the same quality of medical care. Poor people tend to be obese more frequently than the general population and to be less informed about health matters. However, a recent study involving more than 18,000 Vietnam veterans, conducted by Dr. Thomas R. O'Brien and reported in the September 15, 1989, issue of the *Journal of the American Medical Association*, seems to indicate that blacks will get diabetes more frequently than whites regardless of weight or diet. The genetic link, however, remains unproved.

EARLY WARNING SIGNS

Because Type II diabetes is so common, and treatment so effective, it is important that people at risk learn to recognize the symptoms. An individual should also know his or her family's medical history. How many people in the family have the disease? Which ancestors were diagnosed with Type II diabetes? This information should be included in medical records. We would expect that an obese 90-year-old woman whose 4 grandparents had Type II diabetes would have a much greater chance of developing the disease than does an active, thin 18-year-old male whose family shows no incidence of the disease. There is, however, no guarantee, though most people with Type II diabetes are diagnosed after the age of 40 and 80% of them are overweight.

The Medic Alert program. This wrist bracelet and wallet-sized identification card may mean the difference between life and death for a comatose diabetic.

I HAVE DIABETES

If I am unconscious or acting strangely, I may be having a reaction to insulin or to an oral medicine taken for diabetes.

▲ **American Diabetes Association., Inc.**

If I can swallow, give me sugar, candy, fruit juice or a sweetened drink. If I do not recover within 15 minutes or if I cannot swallow, call a physician or send me to a hospital quickly.

Unlike Type I diabetes, Type II diabetes usually develops slowly. It can take years before any symptoms become noticeable. The earliest symptoms may be vague or not seem very important. It is estimated that more than 5 million Americans have diabetes and do not know it. Unfortunately, if not diagnosed and successfully treated, Type II diabetes can lead to serious long-term complications. These are discussed in the next chapter.

Type II diabetes is often called "the great imitator." Early warning signs such as fatigue are common to a large number of illnesses. Some people with Type II diabetes experience the classic symptoms of Type I diabetes: extreme thirst, extreme hunger, and frequent urination. Others may suffer blurred vision or from sores that do not heal quickly. Men may experience impotence, and women may have frequent vaginal infections.

At least 25% of all people diagnosed with Type II diabetes never experience any of these warning signs or are not aware of them if they do occur. Many people find out about their diabetes through routine medical examinations. Anyone who is in a high-risk category should have his or her doctor monitor the blood and urine for abnormal glucose levels at least once a year. Sudden stress such as that brought about by a serious illness or the death of a loved one can trigger Type II diabetes. Once diabetes is suspected, blood glucose and glucose tolerance tests can be used to confirm the diagnosis.

CONTROLLING TYPE II DIABETES

Type II diabetes, like Type I diabetes, cannot be cured, but it can be controlled. For most people with Type II, this will not require insulin injections. For some, just losing weight will reverse insulin resistance and return glucose levels to normal. For many others, maintaining a proper diet and a regular exercise program will keep their diabetes in check.

Unlike Type I diabetes, Type II diabetes can be mild, moderate, or severe, depending on the degree of insulin resistance. It is much easier to correct the disease with diet and exercise if insulin resistance has not reached an advanced state. There are many people, however, who cannot control their weight no matter how hard they try. There are also people with Type II diabetes whose glucose levels remain dangerously high even if their weight is normal and they get regular exercise. Others may need additional help during times of sickness or stress. Fortunately, medical treatment exists for all of these situations.

Pills that improve the body's ability to use insulin were first developed in 1955. Although no one is absolutely certain how they function, most researchers feel they probably stimulate inactive insulin receptors to get back to work. Because they require the presence of insulin and are not a substitute for it, these pills are only effective in treating Type II diabetes. At least six different types of pills are currently on the market, but all are primarily sulfa drugs. They vary in strength and length of effect. For many patients, they provide a successful option for long-term treatment of Type II diabetes. They can also be used on a short-term basis. With newly diagnosed Type II patients, these pills can help normalize glucose levels until diet and exercise programs take control. They can also be used during high stress situations that can temporarily impair receptor functioning.

Although the vast majority of Type II diabetics do not need insulin injections, some do. If glucose levels are dangerously high at the time of diagnosis, insulin injections will often provide the most rapid

Eating a balanced diet and avoiding obesity may be all a person needs to do to control the symptoms of Type II diabetes.

reversal of symptoms. Some Type II diabetics do require long-term insulin injection therapy. Generally, however, because they are producing some insulin, they do not need injections as frequently as do Type I diabetics.

SUDDEN COMPLICATIONS

Monitoring blood glucose levels is as important for Type II diabetics as for Type I diabetics. Regular testing provides the quickest and most accurate measure of how well a person is controlling his or her diabetes. Type II diabetes is generally considered a less serious disease than Type I diabetes. Ketoacidosis, one of the most serious complications of diabetes, very rarely occurs in Type II patients. This is not to say that sudden complications cannot occur. In general, however, they are not as sudden nor as severe.

Many Type II diabetics, particularly those who are able to control glucose levels through diet and exercise, will never experience hypoglycemia, the reaction associated with high insulin levels. Mild hypoglycemia, however, is not uncommon among Type II diabetics treated with pills or insulin. Routine blood tests will usually provide sufficient warning if a crisis situation is building. A change in dosage, a change in timing, or the addition of a snack or two will return glucose levels to normal. Type II diabetics, however, should be aware of the warning signs of hypoglycemia and be prepared with a quick-energy snack to avoid losing consciousness.

Acute hyperglycemia, the reaction associated with high sugar levels, also occurs far less frequently in Type II diabetics than in those with Type I. For patients controlling their diabetes through diet and exercise, hyperglycemia can result from overeating, stress, or eating foods too high in carbohydrates. Type II diabetics on pills or insulin who forget to take their medicine can experience a glucose imbalance. Usually, hyperglycemia will be indicated through the daily monitoring of blood glucose levels. Type II diabetics generally have plenty of time to consult their doctors before glucose levels become dangerously high.

CHAPTER 6

LONG-TERM COMPLICATIONS

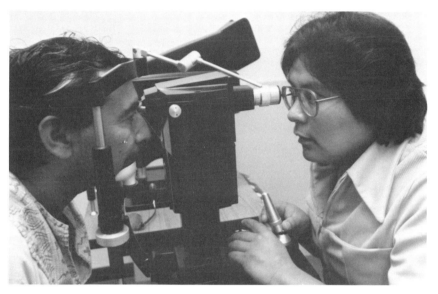

Frequent eye tests are highly recommended for diabetics.

If diabetes is not controlled, excessive glucose in the blood can cause serious problems over time. Nearly all of the body's organs can be damaged. This is why early diagnosis is particularly important. For Type I diabetics, the sudden and dramatic onset of the disease usually results in a quick diagnosis and treatment plan. For Type II diabetics, however, symptoms may develop so slowly that the first indication of diabetes may be the development of a long-term, serious complication.

Type II diabetics can feel fine for two, four, or even more years as the disease gradually progresses. During this time, abnormally high levels of glucose are circulating throughout their bodies causing havoc and destruction. People who are at high risk for developing diabetes should have routine medical tests performed, particularly after the age of 40, regardless of whether or not they experience any symptoms. Once diabetes has been diagnosed, controlling blood glucose will play a crucial role in preventing or delaying the development of long-term complications.

TOO SWEET FOR TOO LONG

What happens over time when glucose levels are too high? The first part of the body usually affected is the circulatory system. This network of large and small blood vessels carries oxygen and nutrients to every cell and removes waste products. If glucose levels are too high, the interior walls of these vessels are bathed continuously with an abnormally high concentration of blood sugar.

High glucose levels encourage fatty deposits to collect inside large blood vessels, such as the arteries that carry blood to the heart and brain. As deposits build up, the vessels become clogged and blood cannot flow through them efficiently. This condition is called *atherosclerosis*. If untreated, total blockage may occur. If this happens in a blood vessel leading to the heart, the individual suffers a heart attack. If the blocked vessel leads to the brain, it causes a stroke. Diabetics have two to four times as great a risk of having a heart attack or stroke as do people without diabetes. Damage to large blood vessels can also result in poor circulation to the legs. The problems caused by long-term damage to major arteries and veins are known as *macrovascular* complications. The majority of diabetes-related deaths are a direct result of this type of damage.

Damage to small blood vessels, such as the tiny capillaries that directly connect to individual cells, causes *microvascular* complications. Over a long period of time, excess glucose can damage these blood vessels as well as large ones. Once this happens, the delivery of oxygen and fuel to the cells begins to break down. Without proper nourishment, cells die and organs malfunction. Eyes, kidneys, and nerves are particularly sensitive to microvascular damage.

Eyes

The loss of sight is a frightening experience to contemplate. For diabetics, this fear is very real. According to the National Eye Institute, diabetics are 25 times more likely to go blind than the general population. Among diabetics, blindness is most often caused by damage to the retina. This is the lining inside the eye at the very back of the organ. When light enters the eye, it travels to the retina. Here, it is directed to the brain by way of the optic nerve.

Damage to the retina caused by diabetes is called *diabetic retinopathy*. It is the most frequent and most serious eye problem caused by diabetes. It is also the most common cause of adult blindness in the United States. Two forms of retinopathy have been identified. The earlier stage is called *background retinopathy*, which occurs when blood vessels within the retina deteriorate. Some vessels shrink. Others enlarge, forming balloon-shaped sacs of blood and fatty tissue called *microaneurysms* that block the flow of blood. The blocked vessels hemorrhage, or bleed, causing the normally thin retina to swell. Sometimes, deposits from the leaking vessels build up on the retina. Although this can cause blurry vision, most people maintain fairly normal sight. Twenty percent of the diabetics who have background retinopathy, however, will eventually develop *proliferative retinopathy*, a far more serious condition.

In proliferative retinopathy, new blood vessels actually grow on the surface of the retina or on the optic nerve. These vessels frequently rupture and bleed into the *vitreous humor*, a clear gelatinous substance that fills up the center of the eye. The blood clouds the vitreous humor and distorts images before they reach the retina. To make matters worse, the exploding blood vessels create scar tissue that further blocks the transfer of images. It can also pull the retina away from the back wall of the eye. If the retina detaches, sudden blindness will occur. A

Monitoring Blood Sugar Levels

Close monitoring of blood sugar levels is very important for most diabetics, certainly for those suffering from Type I diabetes. Control of blood glucose levels is believed to reduce or even reverse the effects of long-term complications—damage to blood vessels and the resulting eye, kidney, and nerve damage. More immediately, monitoring blood sugar can prevent diabetic emergencies such as hyperglycemia and hypoglycemia.

Urine testing is not an acceptable alternative to blood testing. Whereas urine tests will accurately show the presence of ketones, they are highly inaccurate in measuring the presence of sugar in the blood. The sugar level that shows up in urine tests is several hours old at the time of measurement. The rate at which sugar spills into the urine varies and may simply bear no relationship to actual blood sugar levels. Certain chemicals such as aspirin or vitamin C can affect the accuracy of urine tests.

Today there are many different devices on the market to help diabetics test their blood sugar. The test is generally fast, accurate, painless, and can be performed anywhere. The tip of the finger is sterilized with alcohol. Some type of lancet or needle—it may be an automatic, spring-loaded device—pricks the tip of the finger, and a drop of blood is dropped onto a chemically treated piece of paper. The paper will change color, depending on the amount of glucose in the blood. The color of the paper strip is then compared to a color-coded chart, or with the newer test units, the paper strip is read by an electronic device with a digital display, like a small electronic calculator.

The test results are recorded, and over a period of time an individual will learn what his or her normal

glucose level is supposed to be. If readings are abnormal, an adjustment is made to diet, to the dose of insulin, or perhaps to the amount of exercise a person engages in. Tests may be conducted two to four times a day, on a schedule worked out with the help of a doctor. The usual times for testing are before or after meals, in the morning or at bedtime, or before exercise or other vigorous physical activity.

detached retina requires immediate surgery in order for sight to be restored.

In recent years, a significant advance in the treatment of diabetic retinopathy has been developed using powerful laser beams to seal off leaking blood vessels. This therapy, known as *photocoagulation*, can prevent severe vision loss for many patients. An early diagnosis of retinopathy, however, is essential for this treatment to be effective. Usually, by the time symptoms of retinopathy are noticed, some permanent damage has already occurred. It is essential that people diagnosed with diabetes, regardless of age, be referred to an ophthalmologist for a complete eye exam.

Unfortunately, some patients are not good candidates for photocoagulation therapy. Either the retinal damage is too extensive or the amount of bleeding is too great. Sight may sometimes be restored in such cases by a *vitrectomy*, a surgical procedure in which the vitreous humor is totally removed and replaced with a clear, sterile solution.

Over time, excess blood sugar may cause background retinopathy, a deterioration of small blood vessels in the retina of the eye that causes blurred vision.

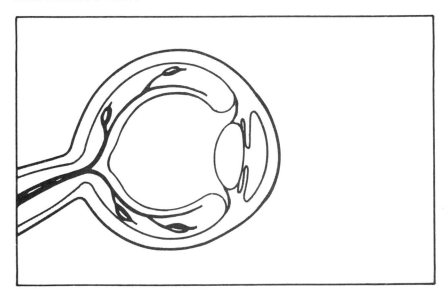

Kidneys

When sugar levels get too high, the kidneys have to work overtime. Excessive urination, which is often the first symptom of diabetes, results from the kidneys' valiantly trying to remove excess sugar from the body. Unfortunately, no matter how hard the kidneys try to filter out excess glucose, if diabetes is untreated, sugar levels stay abnormally high.

Although it usually takes a long time, as long as 20 to 30 years, uncontrolled diabetes can ultimately cause kidney failure. The slow progression of kidney disease probably accounts for the fact that nearly 50% of Type I diabetics experience kidney failure whereas only about 6% of Type II diabetics reach this advanced disease state. As we know, Type I diabetics are usually diagnosed at a much younger age than Type II diabetics and live with their disease much longer.

Diabetic kidney disease is caused by both macrovascular and microvascular problems. Like the heart and brain, the kidneys can be

Background retinopathy may develop into proliferative retinopathy, in which the small blood vessels of the retina rupture and bleed into the vitreous humor. This may lead to blindness.

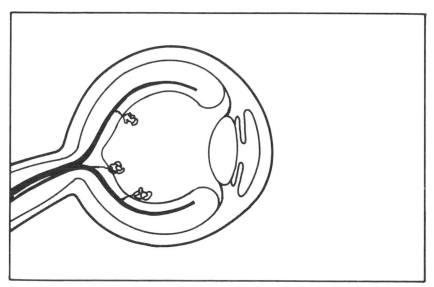

damaged if the large blood vessels that supply them with nutrients become narrowed or clogged. When this happens, the kidneys do not get sufficient food and oxygen and cannot work as efficiently.

The kidneys are also affected by damage to the small blood vessels. Although kidneys are usually less than five inches long and three inches wide, each one has more than a million small blood vessels packed into a clump called the *glomerulus*. The glomerulus has the job of filtering the blood and producing urine. Over time, excess sugar in the blood will damage the walls of the small blood vessels in the glomerulus and they will begin to hemorrhage. This causes a loss of protein as molecules escape from the bloodstream and end up in the urine. It also causes painful swelling as fluids leak into surrounding tissues.

If not caught in time, damage to the glomeruli produces *uremic poisoning* as waste products that should be expelled in the urine build up in the blood. Symptoms of uremic poisoning include fatigue, loss of appetite, and nausea. People cannot live without functioning kidneys. Once 95% of the glomeruli have been damaged, death will result unless the person is routinely treated with an artificial kidney machine or receives a kidney transplant. Although there is no cure for diabetic kidney disease, advances are being made in preventing or slowing progressive damage.

Nerves

The nervous system coordinates all bodily activity through three main networks. The *cranial nerves* service the head; the *autonomic nerves* control the functions of our internal organs; and the *peripheral nerves* branch out from the brain and spinal column to both transmit sensations and control the voluntary muscles of the body. A problem with the nervous system caused by diabetes is called *diabetic neuropathy*.

Diabetes can affect nerve function by damaging the small blood vessels that feed the nerve cells. The disease also interferes with the transmission of neural impulses by damaging the thin layer of fat that surrounds and protects the nerves. When fat is stripped from nerves, the effect is just as if electrical wires have lost their insulation: The transmission of signals goes haywire.

The peripheral nerves of the feet and hands seem to be damaged most frequently. The resulting problems may be temporary or chronic, and a variety of unpleasant symptoms can occur: a tingling sensation or numbness, or severe, burning pain. Although numbness may at first seem like the lesser evil, diabetics may hurt themselves without knowing it because they are unable to feel sensations in their hands or feet. Serious infections can go unnoticed. There is currently no treatment available for neuropathy involving numbness or tingling.

Painful neuropathy generally occurs in bouts lasting from 6 to 18 months. Although doctors are not sure why they work, antidepressants and drugs used to prevent seizures seem to reduce pain for many people.

Cranial neuropathy is usually temporary. Symptoms include double vision or facial paralysis. Autonomic neuropathy can cause diarrhea, constipation, and impotence. Although the first two can usually be successfully treated, impotence caused by diabetes is rarely reversible.

Most doctors agree that maintaining control of glucose levels is the best prevention for all forms of diabetic neuropathy.

Feet

The feet of diabetics are very susceptible to injury. Damage to peripheral arteries can restrict blood flow. Without sufficient oxygen and nutrients, the cells of the feet cannot effectively fight off infection or heal properly. If neuropathy is present, the feet may become numb. In the worst cases, gangrene can occur. This involves the extensive death of tissue as bacteria from an infection spread wildly. If unchecked, amputation may be necessary. Approximately 50,000 below-the-knee amputations are performed each year on diabetics, according to the Centers for Disease Control in Atlanta.

Most foot problems can be avoided through a program of daily care. New shoes should be chosen carefully for maximum comfort to avoid blisters and calluses. People with diabetes should avoid walking barefoot. Feet should be protected from exposure to extreme heat or cold. Diabetics should inspect their feet every day and seek medical attention immediately if any problems are noted. Feet should be kept clean, and nails should be cut straight across to prevent ingrown toenails.

REDUCING THE RISK

Early diagnosis of diabetes, effective control, and a greater awareness of potential problems can eliminate or at least slow the progression of long-term complications.

Keeping blood pressure within normal limits is crucial. High blood pressure, also known as *hypertension*, is deadly. With or without diabetes, it is an important risk factor for heart disease. For the diabetic, high blood pressure frequently causes both heart problems and kidney disease.

Obesity, a primary cause of Type II diabetes, and atherosclerosis promote hypertension. Cigarette smoking compounds the damage. Chemicals in cigarettes constrict blood vessels. As they narrow, blood pressure rises.

Excessive stress, a primary factor in high blood pressure, should be recognized and avoided. Too much stress can also drastically affect blood sugar levels, making it much more difficult for diabetics to keep their glucose level under control.

The best way to minimize the dangers of diabetes is to take good care of oneself. For the most part, this involves the same advice, knowledge, and goals that everyone uses to stay well. For the diabetic who wants to live a normal life, however, a healthy life-style must be a number one priority.

CHAPTER 7

LIVING WELL
WITH DIABETES

Senators, schoolteachers, doctors, carpenters, actors, and athletes all include diabetics among their ranks. These are people who successfully control their diabetes rather than letting it control them.

Unlike almost any other disease, diabetes demands that the individual take primary responsibility for his or her own health. This requires information, action, and commitment. For the diabetic, living a normal life requires the routine monitoring of blood glucose levels, eating properly, and exercising regularly. For all Type I diabetics and some Type II diabetics, medication is also necessary.

DIET

For diabetics, attention to diet must be a lifetime commitment. The dietary goals for Type I and Type II diabetics differ somewhat. For young Type I diabetics, sufficient calories must be consumed to allow normal, healthy growth. For all Type I diabetics, meals and snacks must be carefully scheduled to match peak periods of insulin activity. For Type II diabetics, the primary challenge is fat. Most Type II diabetics are overweight, and these excess pounds are often what triggered their diabetes. For most Type II diabetics, removing excess weight and keeping it off is all that is necessary to control the disease.

All diabetics need to minimize fat, sugar, and salt in their diet and to eat nutritional meals. A system of meal planning called the *exchange system* has been developed by the American Diabetes Association and the American Dietetic Association. In this system, all foods are categorized according to whether they are primarily starch/bread, meat, vegetable, fruit, milk, or fat. Each category contains a large variety of foods and a recommended portion. This portion becomes the basic unit, or *exchange*. Within each group, each listing is about equal in the number of calories it contains.

With the help of a dietitian, meals are planned based on food groups. For example, a typical lunch may include two starches, two meats, one vegetable, one fruit, one milk, and one fat. This is the formula. What is actually eaten, however, is up to the individual. For example, one meat exchange could be two ounces of roast beef or one-half cup of tuna or salmon. As long as only the recommended amounts and exchange units of food are consumed, the freedom of choice is considerable.

When eating in restaurants, diabetics can make wise choices by asking questions about how dishes are prepared and by resisting the temptation to eat rich or sweet foods. Even eating at fast-food restaurants can be done with confidence, particularly if options such as salads or baked potatoes are offered. It is also good to pick places that cater to special orders.

An excellent introduction to the exchange system is provided in the booklet *Exchange Lists for Meal Planning*, available from the

American Diabetes Association and the American Dietetic Association.

Working with a dietitian, diabetics can develop a meal plan that meets their needs without being boring. The more diabetics learn about food and nutrition, the easier it gets. Of course, attitude is also important. It is difficult for any dieter, but particularly for a young diabetic, to accept the notion that certain foods are not healthy and must be avoided for life. The discipline required to take daily insulin injections and keep accurate records of daily blood tests is wearying for the young person who only wants to live a normal life like all his or her friends. Nutritional discipline requires a lot of support from relatives and friends.

ALCOHOL

Although alcoholic drinks are very high in calories, they have no nutritional value. One shot of 80-proof liquor averages almost 100 calories, a beer has 170, and a glass of wine has 90. One diabetic patient who was very good at maintaining his food intake at 1,200 calories a day could not figure out why his weight and his diabetes were out of control. After extensive questioning by his doctor, the patient mentioned that he was consuming nearly a case of beer a day. Once the patient stopped drinking beer, his weight dropped, his glucose levels returned to normal, and he no longer needed pills for his diabetes.

This is not to say that people with diabetes cannot drink. If the diabetes is under control, a drink before dinner or a glass of wine or beer with dinner should be no problem. The calories must be counted, however, as well as the exchange units. Most alcoholic drinks count as two fats.

For the diabetic, there are some additional considerations regarding alcohol consumption. The symptoms of mild intoxication are very similar to those of hypoglycemia. If a person has had several drinks and simultaneously experiences a reaction to excess insulin, people might not be able to recognize the true nature of the problem. Diabetics must also be careful that drinking does not interfere with the timing of their meals or their medication. For some people, the combination of alcohol and sulfa drugs can cause flushing, a racing heart, or nausea.

MARIJUANA

Aside from being illegal in all 50 states, smoking marijuana can cause serious problems for the diabetic. It is known to alter a person's judgment, and under the influence of marijuana, a person may delay taking necessary medication or may eat improperly. Many people experience a craving for food, especially sweets, after smoking marijuana. Although detrimental to anyone's diet, uncontrolled snacking can be devastating to a diabetic as it can result in weight gain and hyperglycemia.

THE IMPORTANCE OF EXERCISE

A regular exercise program offers health advantages to nearly everyone, regardless of age. Fitness provides flexibility, adds to muscle strength, and improves the efficiency of the heart and lungs. It also provides psychological benefits and helps keep weight down.

Because of its effectiveness in lowering blood glucose levels, exercise has been called the "invisible insulin." An active body uses more glucose than an inactive one. When a person exercises, the cells of the body demand additional fuel, which they get from glucose in the bloodstream. Once these supplies are exhausted, the body draws upon stored glucose. Exercise also increases the sensitivity of insulin receptors, which work better and faster. Available insulin is put to use more efficiently, causing glucose levels to decrease. Many Type I diabetics find that the amount of insulin they require daily decreases once a regular exercise program begins.

Before beginning any exercise program, all diabetics should consult with their doctors. For Type I diabetics, it is crucial that blood sugar levels be tested before and after exercise. If blood glucose is too high, additional insulin may be necessary before exercise. If blood glucose levels fall too low, an additional snack may have to be added to the

Marijuana, alcohol, and other drugs present special problems for diabetics, who must never relax their control over diet and medication. Marijuana may induce a craving for food, especially sweets, which for diabetics can be devastating.

daily diet. By working with their physicians, Type I diabetics can coordinate meals and exercise with peak insulin activity. By frequently monitoring their glucose level, Type I diabetics can achieve all of the benefits of exercise without compromising control of the disease.

In preparing for an exercise program, diabetics must be especially careful when choosing athletic shoes. Because diabetics so often have trouble with their feet, they must make sure they are using appropriate and comfortable footgear at all times.

HOW NORMAL IS NORMAL?

Diabetics who have their disease under control can approach day-to-day activities with confidence. But what about special occasions that can interfere with well-established schedules? A senior prom, a special birthday celebration, or some other important event can cause quite a bit of excitement and anxiety. Such a situation probably means a much later night than usual. Alcoholic beverages may be consumed. The scheduling of meals may be disrupted, and what will be available to eat may be a great mystery.

By planning ahead, diabetics can have just as much fun as anyone else. Insulin and medications should be taken along, as well as monitoring equipment to measure blood sugar levels. A small box of raisins or candy should be available to provide instant relief if too much activity or insufficient food at appropriate times causes hypoglycemia. When food is served, diabetics should avoid sweets and select those items that best fit their daily meal. Close friends should be alerted to watch for any sort of unusual behavior. As for alcohol, abstinence is best, but a person may drink if he or she uses extreme caution. The best time to have a drink would be close to or just after a meal. Checking blood sugar levels before and after taking a drink is also a good idea.

Vacations, overnight trips, and even long excursions can be taken with ease if diabetics plan ahead. They should always have sufficient supplies of insulin and snacks with them. They should attempt to keep their eating and sleeping schedules as normal as possible. They should also monitor blood sugar levels routinely.

A diabetic student who plans on attending college away from home should tell his or her doctor, who can recommend a specialist in the college town, make an initial contact, and make sure that all medical records are transferred. By the time they are ready for college, most diabetics have had at least several years to get their disease under control. The more personal responsibility they take during high school, the easier it will be to maintain control away from parents and home. Diabetic students should not live alone their first year away at school, and they should inform roommates and friends of their condition. Many students will find that their classmates already have firsthand experience with diabetics. This is at least one advantage of having a disease that affects many millions of people.

LOVE, SEX, AND BABIES

For most men and women, having diabetes does not interfere with sexual desire or enjoyment. Although some men may experience diabetes-related impotence, this is fairly unusual and generally takes several decades to develop. Most young diabetics reach puberty and develop sexually at the same rate as their friends. Diabetic men generally maintain a normal sperm count throughout their lives. Women whose diabetes is under control experience normal menstrual cycles and have no unusual difficulties becoming pregnant. There is no reason to assume that diabetes will make a person sterile.

Diabetic women have almost an equal chance of having a successful pregnancy as do women without diabetes. Stabilizing glucose levels before conception and keeping them normal throughout the pregnancy will protect the health of both the mother-to-be and the baby. Diabetic women who are planning to have children should discuss this well in advance with their doctor. They should also be prepared to visit their doctor frequently throughout their pregnancy.

Diabetic women can use almost any form of birth control without additional risk. IUDs, however, are generally not recommended. They are known to cause infections, particularly in women who have not given birth before. Because diabetics have a tendency to bruise more easily and have a harder time fighting infections, an IUD is generally not the wisest choice.

This newborn baby's mother developed diabetes during pregnancy, but new blood-testing devices make it easier for doctors to control glucose levels even with very young infants.

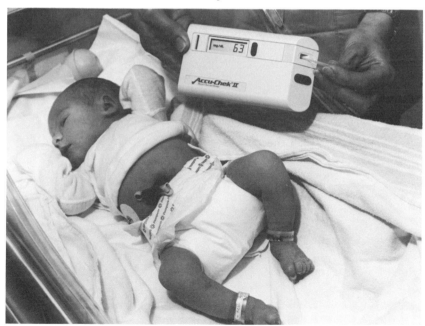

Pregnancy increases the body's need for insulin. As a result, diabetes does develop in 1% to 3% of all women who become pregnant. This form of diabetes is called *gestational diabetes*. Women who get gestational diabetes will usually return to normal after their baby is delivered, but about half of them will become diabetic again later on in life. The American Diabetes Association recommends that all women be tested for diabetes sometime after the 24th week of their pregnancy.

LIMITS AND LICENSE

Can people with diabetes drive a car? Certainly. In every state, diabetics are driving. They must pass the same examinations and driving tests that everyone else takes to obtain a license, and some states do require a doctor's letter stating that the diabetes is under control. A federal regulation prevents insulin-dependent diabetics from being licensed to drive commercial vehicles engaged in interstate or foreign business. Insulin-dependent diabetics are also not allowed to hold a pilot's license.

When driving, diabetics should always have an emergency supply of sugar with them in the car. They should never skip a meal or continue on the road if they begin to feel any of the symptoms of diabetic complications.

It is important for young people with diabetes to know that they are not alone. Support groups are very common among sufferers of this disease and may include other young people, doctors, parents, and social workers.

IDENTIFICATION SAVES LIVES

In 1956, a doctor in California founded a nonprofit company called Medic Alert. His goal was to provide identification for diabetics and other people with serious medical conditions. Medic Alert provides members with a bracelet or necklace engraved with their specific health risks as well as ID cards for their wallets. Medic Alert also maintains a 24-hour emergency telephone hot line that can furnish each member's complete medical history. Members pay only a modest initial fee, and free memberships are provided to people who cannot afford to join. For more information, call 1-800-ID ALERT.

Many diabetics owe their lives to the Medic Alert system. Even diabetics whose disease is under control should carry some form of medical ID at all times. In case of an automobile accident or medical emergency where consciousness may be lost, the proper ID will alert health care workers. For those subject to frequent insulin reactions, it can mean life or death. Having proper ID is just one more way in which diabetics can confidently participate in the world at their full potential.

CAREER PLANNING

There are very few career choices closed to diabetics. In fact, the Federal Rehabilitation Act of 1973 protects diabetics from employment discrimination in all departments and branches of the federal government, the postal system, and in all companies that do more than $2,500 in business with the federal government. Many states also have passed specific antidiscrimination legislation. Some limitations, however, do exist. Insulin-dependent diabetics are still not permitted to enter any branch of the armed forces.

Although almost any career is open to a diabetic, some choices may be wiser than others. A job with regular hours and modest levels of stress may be more conducive to keeping diabetes under control. Although there are diabetic police officers, flight attendants, and cardiologists, people choosing these careers must prepare for frequent and often abrupt changes in schedules and higher on-the-job stress.

LEARNING MORE

The American Diabetes Association (ADA) can offer diabetics and their families invaluable information and emotional support. Local chapters exist throughout the United States to provide members with classes, discussion groups, medical referrals, and advice on such topics as jobs, insurance, and health care. The ADA also has more than 100 publications available at little or no cost providing the latest information on every aspect of living well with diabetes. The organization also publishes a monthly magazine called *Forecast* for "people with diabetes who want to live healthier and happier lives."

The ADA is active in funding diabetes research directly and in making sure that government funds are available to continue this work. The telephone numbers of local branches can be found in the phone book under American Diabetes Association, or one can call 1-800-ADA-DISC to speak to someone in the national office.

The Juvenile Diabetes Foundation is an international, nonprofit organization active in funding research as well as in providing information for diabetic children and their families. This organization is located in New York and can be reached by calling 1-212-889-7575.

The National Diabetes Information Clearinghouse, funded by the federal government and with headquarters in Maryland, is an organization dedicated to increasing knowledge about the disease among diabetics, health care workers, and the public. The clearinghouse also provides many valuable publications as well as maintaining an on-line computer data base. More information about this agency can be obtained by calling 1-301-468-2162.

CHAPTER 8

RECENT PROGRESS AND FUTURE GOALS

The modern insulin pump

The quality of life now available to people with diabetes is one of medicine's greatest success stories. There have been important advances in controlling the disease, preventing complications, and treating problems that develop. Genetic engineering makes human insulin widely available. Easy-to-use, accurate blood glucose tests help prevent hypoglycemia and hyperglycemia. Knowledge about nutrition and exercise allows millions to keep their diabetes in check. Laser therapy can save the eyesight of thousands of diabetics with retinopathy. Diabetic women can now approach pregnancy and childbirth with confidence. Now that diabetes can be controlled, efforts are shifting to a search for an effective cure. The cure for diabetes will probably require two separate approaches, one for each type of the disease. Although scientists are uncertain as to the exact cause of either Type I or Type II diabetes, they are fairly confident that different agents are involved.

In investigating the cause of Type I diabetes, researchers are studying the genes of the beta cells. Why are beta cells in diabetics so easily destroyed compared to the beta cells of healthy individuals? Are Type I diabetics missing a crucial gene? Do they have an extra gene that doesn't belong? Do they have damaged genes or genes in the wrong positions? These are some of the questions scientists are asking. As genetic engineering advances, repairing or replacing damaged genes may become a reality.

The search for a cure for Type II diabetes presents a different set of problems. Which genes are involved? Can insulin resistance be prevented? Is there more than one cause of Type II diabetes? Why is obesity such an important risk factor?

TRIAL AND ERROR

Most medical experts agree that Type I diabetes is caused by an autoimmune reaction. If this could be stopped, Type I diabetes could be prevented. Obviously, one way to stop the immune system from attacking the beta cells is to shut it down entirely. Drugs are available

Designed to look like a fountain pen, the NovolinPen is a new, high-tech, self-contained syringe that comes with disposable needles and replaceable insulin cartridges.

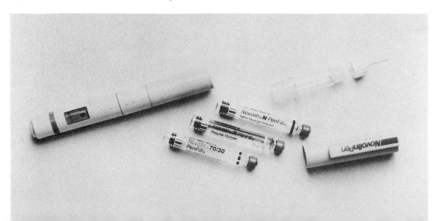

that can accomplish this. These immunosuppressive drugs were developed for organ transplant patients. Before and after a transplant, they are administered to suppress the immune response and prevent the body from rejecting the new organ.

In experiments with Type I diabetics, it was found that these same drugs could effectively reverse damage to beta cells and prevent healthy beta cells from being destroyed. The sooner diabetes was detected and therapy started, the better the effect.

Unfortunately, immunosuppressive drugs are very expensive and very dangerous. If used for long periods of time they can cause serious kidney damage. They also make it nearly impossible for the body to fight off any infection. Although these drugs are not the magic cure for Type I diabetes, they offer encouragement and direction for the development of equally effective but less dangerous agents.

BETA CELLS IN SPACE

Scientists are also working on the replacement of damaged beta cells by transplanting either beta cells or an entire pancreas. These studies are highly experimental. For a beta cell transplant to succeed, beta cells must be removed from a healthy pancreas and implanted into a diabetic pancreas. They also have to be protected from the destructive agents that killed the original beta cells. These are not easy tasks. Just harvesting healthy cells is a challenge. Orbiting space stations may prove to be the best laboratories of the future for this procedure. At zero gravity, beta cells seem to separate more readily.

Experiments are also under way to keep the beta cells alive following transplantation. Researchers are trying to develop a protective capsule to enclose the beta cells. It will have holes large enough to allow glucose in and insulin out but not large enough to admit lethal killer cells. So far, beta cell transplants have been performed only on animals and the success of these operations has been limited.

Pancreas transplants are also in their infancy, although these are now being performed on humans. Unfortunately, the benefits do not seem to last very long. Most people who receive pancreas transplants regain control of blood glucose levels for only a year or less.

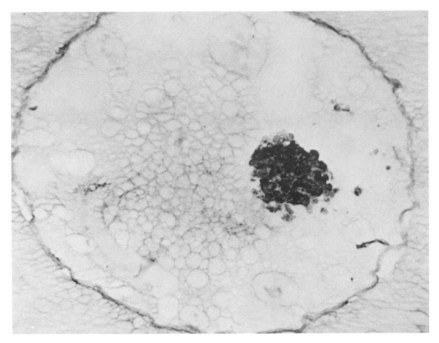

Living, insulin-producing beta cells encased in a capsule a half-millimeter in diameter, designed to protect the cells from digestive enzymes. If this bold new invention proves successful, diabetics may no longer need their syringes and needles.

TAKING WHAT WORKS AND MAKING IT BETTER

Until diabetes can be cured, the administration of insulin will remain the primary treatment technique for all Type I diabetics and also for some Type II diabetics who need the hormone.

A major goal of medical research in this field is to eliminate the necessity for injections. Unfortunately, insulin is destroyed by stomach acids, so it cannot be taken orally. Dr. Bernard Ecanow, a retired professor of pharmaceutical science at the University of Illinois, is working on this problem. Dr. Ecanow is developing a protective casing for insulin made out of microscopic droplets of water hardened to the consistency of gelatin. Within these protective droplets, insulin can resist digestive enzymes and reach the bloodstream. Although preliminary studies with animals are encouraging, much additional research will have to be performed to see if this will work effectively for humans.

THE INSULIN PUMP

Insulin pumps were developed in the 1970s. Worn on the outside of the body, they deliver insulin through a tube attached to a needle penetrating the skin. The pumps are battery operated and about the size of a pack of cards. The amount of insulin they deliver is controlled through a keyboard by the person wearing the pump. Some people prefer pumps to injections, especially diabetics who require insulin frequently during the day. Others find the pumps to be more of a problem than they are worth. The pump's batteries have to be changed frequently, as well as the connecting tubing and needle. The insulin reservoir has to be refilled and the controls reprogrammed. Pump users must test their glucose level even more often than other insulin-dependent diabetics to make sure the pump is working. With the right attitude and care, however, insulin pumps can go just about everywhere.

Most medical experts agree that the best method of controlling insulin delivery would be to make it automatic. This would require a system to continually measure blood glucose levels and respond with appropriate doses of insulin release. In other words, it would mimic the action of a healthy pancreas. Ideally, this system could be worn internally much like a pacemaker. Researchers are hard at work to make this a reality. They are developing both a glucose sensor that can work internally and a pump that can be tolerated inside the body for long periods of time.

THE BEST IS YET TO COME

The future for diabetics looks brighter each decade. In coming years, further advances will likely be made to make treatment easier and more effective. Diabetes research offers many exciting challenges and op-

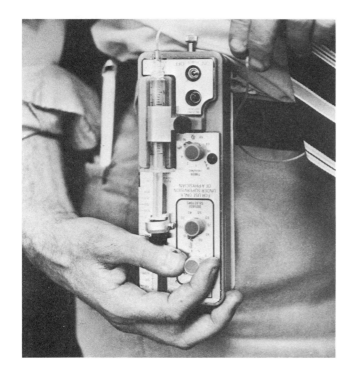

An early-model insulin pump, circa 1980. This bulky device was designed to eliminate the diabetic's need for daily injections by automatically squirting small amounts of insulin into the skin. Newer models are no larger than a hockey puck.

portunities for those interested in careers in medical research. By working together to fight diabetes, concerned citizens can help the millions of people around the world who have the disease and can hasten a cure for future generations.

APPENDIX I

Healthy Recipes for Diabetics

The following recipes from the Nutrition Consultation Service at New York Hospital in Manhattan are examples of nutritious low-sugar meal choices available to people with diabetes. The "exchanges" (see Chapter 7) per serving of each of the following recipes is included below.

Sesame-Peanut Pasta

Ingredients: 1/3 cup crunchy peanut butter
1 teaspoon sesame seed oil
1 teaspoon sesame seeds
2 teaspoons cider vinegar
1 tablespoon chopped green onion
  dash cayenne pepper
3 tablespoons cold water
3 ounces spaghetti
1 quart water

Directions: Mix together peanut butter, sesame seed oil, sesame seeds, vinegar, green onion, and cayenne pepper. Beat cold water into the mixture a little at a time, using a fork, until sauce thickens. Cook spaghetti in 1 quart boiling water for about 15 minutes. Drain well. Sauce and pasta may be served hot or cold.

Makes: 2 servings

Serving Size: 1/4 cup sauce combined with 3/4 cup spaghetti

Per Serving: Calories = 441
Carbohydrates = 40 grams
Protein = 17 grams
Fat = 25 grams
Sodium = 269 milligrams

Exchanges: 2 starch/breads
2 medium-fat meats
2 fats

Vegetable Pie

Ingredients: 2 cups zucchini, sliced and quartered
1 1/2 cups diced tomatoes
1/2 cup chopped onion
1/2 cup grated parmesan cheese
1/4 teaspoon pepper
1 1/2 cups skim milk
3/4 cup biscuit mix (Bisquick-type)
3 eggs

Directions: Preheat oven to 400 degrees Fahrenheit. Lightly grease an 8- or 9-inch pie pan. Place zucchini, tomatoes, and onions in bottom of pan. Sprinkle parmesan cheese and pepper evenly over vegetables. Blend together milk, biscuit mix, and eggs until smooth and pour mixture over vegetables. Bake for 30 minutes. Let sit about 5 minutes before serving.

Makes: 6 servings

Serving Size: 1/6 of pie

Per Serving: Calories = 177
Carbohydrates = 18 grams
Protein = 10 grams
Fat = 7 grams
Sodium = 387 milligrams

Exchanges: 2 vegetables
1/2 starch/bread
1 medium-fat meat

Mini Pizza

Ingredients: 1 English muffin, split and lightly toasted
4 teaspoons tomato sauce
1/2 cup shredded, part-skim mozzarella cheese
1 teaspoon oregano
1 teaspoon basil

Directions: Spread each side of muffin with 2 teaspoons tomato sauce, 1/4 cup mozzarella cheese, 1/2 teaspoon oregano, and 1/2 teaspoon basil. Broil until cheese melts. Serve immediately.

Makes: 2 servings

Serving Size: 1 pizza

Per Serving: Calories = 135
Carbohydrates = 15 grams
Protein = 10 grams
Fat = 3 grams
Sodium = 295 milligrams

Exchanges: 1 starch/bread
1 lean meat

Whole Wheat Pancakes

Ingredients: 1 cup whole wheat flour
2 teaspoons baking powder
1/2 teaspoon vanilla
1/4 teaspoon salt
1 cup lowfat milk
1 egg
1 tablespoon vegetable oil

Directions: Mix together dry ingredients. Add remaining ingredients and mix until blended. Drop 2 tablespoons onto a hot, lightly greased griddle. Cook until bubbles form on top and edges appear dry. Flip and cook until lightly brown.

Makes: 6 servings

Serving Size: 2 pancakes

Per Serving: Calories = 118
Carbohydrates = 17 grams
Protein = 5 grams
Fat = 4 grams
Sodium = 263 milligrams

Exchanges: 1 starch/bread
1 fat

Breakfast Shake

Ingredients: 2 ripe bananas
1 cup skim milk
1/2 cup plain nonfat yogurt
1/4 cup wheat germ
2 teaspoons vanilla
1 packet sugar substitute (optional)

Directions: Freeze bananas overnight. Combine all ingredients in blender and mix until smooth. Serve immediately.

Makes: 2 servings

Serving Size: 1 1/4 cup

Per Serving: Calories = 264
Carbohydrates = 40 grams
Protein = 15 grams
Fat = 6 grams
Sodium = 142 milligrams

Exchanges: 1 nonfat milk
2 fruits
1 starch/bread
1 fat

Fried Chicken

Ingredients: 6 chicken breast halves, skin removed
18 saltine crackers, crushed
2 tablespoons grated parmesan cheese
3/4 teaspoon pepper
1/2 teaspoon basil
1/2 teaspoon onion powder
1/2 teaspoon oregano
1/2 teaspoon paprika
3/8 teaspoon salt
1/4 cup evaporated skim milk
1 tablespoon vegetable oil

Directions: Combine cracker crumbs, parmesan cheese, pepper, basil, onion powder, oregano, paprika, and salt in mixing bowl. Dip chicken in evaporated milk and then roll in crumb mixture until evenly coated. Place chicken in lightly greased, shallow baking pan and bake at 400 degrees Fahrenheit for 30 minutes. Lightly brush chicken with oil and bake for 10 more minutes at same temperature.

Makes: 6 servings

Serving Size: 1/2 breast

Per Serving: Calories = 260
Carbohydrates = 7 grams
Protein = 31 grams
Fat = 11 grams
Sodium = 351 milligrams

Exchanges: 1/2 starch/bread
3 lean meats
1/2 fat

Trail Mix Snack

Ingredients: 2 dried apple rings
3 tablespoons raisins
2 tablespoons peanuts
2 tablespoons sunflower seeds
2 tablespoons unsweetened shredded coconut
1 tablespoon semisweet mini chocolate chips

Directions: Cut apple rings into small pieces. Mix ingredients together. Store in airtight container.

Makes: 2 servings

Serving Size: One half of batch

Per Serving: Calories = 216
Carbohydrates = 22 grams
Protein = 15 grams
Fat = 12 grams
Sodium = 55 milligrams

Exchanges: 1 starch/bread
2 fats
1 fruit

APPENDIX II

Insulin-related Illness

The following are causes and symptoms of, as well as treatments for, the potentially serious, even fatal, ailments that can strike insulin-dependent diabetics.

Hypoglycemia

Cause:

> Too little glucose in the blood to accommodate the amount of insulin taken by the patient

Symptoms:

> Irritability
> Pale, moist skin
> Sweating
> Dizziness
> Rapid pulse
> Feeling of weakness
> Faintness
> Poor concentration
> Feeling of confusion
> Lack of coordination
> Headache
> Fatigue
> Nausea
> Stomach pains

Treatment:

> Sugar taken immediately in the form of, for example, the following:
> Nondiet soft drink
> Orange juice
> Candy
> Glucose tablets
> Small box of raisins

If the diabetic is unconscious, call an ambulance, and if possible, the patient should receive an injection of glucagon (provided that someone experienced in administering the prescription drug is present) before the paramedics arrive. Glucagon will change sugar stored in the liver into glucose.

Always contact a physician after a severe hypoglycemic reaction, even if home treatment is successful.

Hyperglycemia

Cause:

Too little insulin in the bloodstream

Symptoms:

Often occur slowly and can include the following:
Extreme thirst
Frequent urination
Irritability
Frequent infections

Treatment:

A proper meal plan and a sufficient supply of insulin. If hyper-glycemia is untreated, a patient may develop ketoacidosis.

Ketoacidosis

Cause:

Lack of insulin to help burn sugar, forcing the body to instead break down fat for energy. This results in the release of a toxic quantity of ketones into the bloodstream.

Symptoms:

Extreme thirst
Frequent urination
Fruity odor on breath
Sudden, severe weight loss
Nausea and vomiting
Stomach pains
Unconsciousness (diabetic coma)

Treatment:

A physician must be contacted immediately or, if the doctor is unavailable, the patient should be taken to the nearest hospital emergency room.

If untreated, ketoacidosis can cause death.

APPENDIX III:
FOR MORE INFORMATION

The following is a list of organizations that can provide information on issues related to diabetes and its treatment.

GENERAL

American Association of Diabetes
  Educators
500 North Michigan Avenue
Suite 1400
Chicago, IL 60611
(312) 667-1700

Barnes Hospital
Division of Health Education
One Barnes Hospital Plaza
St. Louis, MO 63110
(314) 362-1390

Canadian Diabetes Association
78 Bond Street
Toronto, Ontario M5B 2J8
Canada
(416) 362-4440

City of Hope National Medical Center
Diabetes Educational Office
1500 East Durate Road
Durate, CA 91010
(818) 359-8111

Diabetes and Metabolism Clinic
Stanford University Medical Center
Room S-005
Stanford, CA 94305
(415) 723-6054

Joslin Diabetes Center
One Joslin Place
Boston, MA 02215
(617) 732-2400

Juvenile Diabetes Foundation
  International
432 Park Avenue South
New York, NY 10016
(212) 889-7575
Hot Line: (800) JDS-CURE

National Diabetes Information
  Clearinghouse
Box NDIC
Bethesda, MD 20205
(301) 468-2162

National Health and Information Center
Office of Disease Prevention and Health
  Promotion

P.O. Box 1133
Washington, DC 20013
(301) 565-4167 (in Washington)
(800) 336-4797

University of Alabama in Birmingham
Diabetes Research and Training Center
1808 Seventh Avenue South
Birmingham, AL 35294
(205) 934-3019

University of Virginia
Diabetes and Metabolism Center
Charlottesville, VA 22908
(804) 924-1825

DIABETIC RETINOPATHY

National Society to Prevent Blindness
160 East 56th Street
New York, NY 10022
(212) 980-2020

ENDOCRINOLOGY

Canadian Society of Endocrinology
  and Metabolism
Montreal General Hospital
Room 7823-2H
1650 Cedar Avenue
Montreal, Quebec H3G 1A4
Canada
(514) 934-8017

Endocrinology Society
9650 Rockville Pike
Bethesda, MD 20814
(301) 571-1802

International Society of Endocrinology
Department of Chemical Endocrinology
St. Bartholomew's Hospital
51-53 Bartholomew Close

London, EC1A 7BEUK
England
01-606-4012

Larson Wilkins Pediatric
  Endocrine Society
Department of Endocrinology
Children's National Medical Center
111 Michigan Avenue NW
Washington, DC 20010
(202) 745-2121

HYPOGLYCEMIA

Adrenal Metabolic Research Society
  of the Hypoglycemia Foundation
153 Pawling Avenue
Troy, NY 12180
(518) 272-7154

Dr. John W. Tintera Memorial
Hypoglycemia Lay Group (HLG)
149 Spindle Road
Hicksville, NY 11801
(516) 731-3302

THE AMERICAN DIABETES ASSOCIATION

The American Diabetes Association
(ADA) was founded in 1940 with the
dual purpose of easing the suffering of
diabetics and promoting the search for
an eventual cure. It conducts fund-rais-
ing efforts and lobbies government legis-
lators to make contributions to medical
research. It promotes public awareness
of the disease and provides educational
services to medical professionals as well
as diabetics. It forms support groups to
help diabetics deal with the difficult
physical and emotional problems of
never being able to relax their vigilance
over diet and medication. The ADA

publishes numerous pamphlets and its monthly magazine, *Diabetes Forecast.* Some of this material is created for specific groups with special problems, such as children and teenagers. Other publications include meal plans based on the ADA's *exchange list* system, which teaches diabetics how to make their diet varied and interesting. The ADA has a national office in Virginia and maintains offices in all 50 states, and can be contacted for more information at the following locations:

American Diabetes Association
National Service Center
1660 Duke Street
Alexandria, VA 22314
(703) 549-1500
Hot Line: (800) ADA-DISC

STATE LISTING

ALABAMA

Alabama Affiliate, Inc.
P.O. Box 360253
Birmingham, AL 35236
(205) 326-9995

ALASKA

Alaska Affiliate, Inc.
4241 B Street
Room 102
Anchorage, AK 99503
(907) 563-3607

ARIZONA

Arizona Affiliate, Inc.
P.O. Box 37579
Phoenix, AZ 85069
(602) 995-1515

ARKANSAS

Arkansas Affiliate, Inc.
The Executive Suite Building
Suite 19
Little Rock, AR 72212
(501) 221-7444

CALIFORNIA

Northern California Affiliate, Inc.
2550 9th Street
Suite 114
Berkeley, CA 94710
(415) 644-0920

Southern California Affiliate, Inc.
3460 Wilshire Boulevard
Suite 900
Los Angeles, CA 90010
(213) 381-3639

COLORADO

Colorado Affiliate, Inc.
2450 South Downing Street
Denver, CO 80210
(303) 778-7556

CONNECTICUT

Connecticut Affiliate, Inc.
40 South Street
West Hartford, CT 06110
(203) 953-4232

DELAWARE

Delaware Affiliate, Inc.
2713 Lancaster Avenue
Wilmington, DE 19805
(302) 656-0030

DISTRICT OF COLUMBIA

Washington, D.C. Area Affiliate, Inc.

1211 Connecticut Avenue
Suite 501
Washington, DC 20036
(202) 331-8303

FLORIDA

Florida Affiliate, Inc.
3101 Maguire Boulevard
Orlando, FL 32803
(407) 894-3888

GEORGIA

Georgia Affiliate, Inc.
3783 Presidential Parkway
Suite 102
Atlanta, GA 30340
(404) 454-8401

HAWAII

Hawaii Affiliate, Inc.
510 South Beretania Street
Honolulu, HI 96813
(808) 521-5677

IDAHO

Idaho Affiliate, Inc.
1528 Vista
Boise, ID 83705
(208) 342-2774

ILLINOIS

Downstate Illinois Affiliate, Inc.
250 Federal Drive
Suite 403
Decatur, IL 62526
(217) 875-9011

Northern Illinois Affiliate, Inc.
6 North Michigan Avenue
Suite 1202

Chicago, IL 60602
(312) 346-1805

INDIANA

Indiana Affiliate, Inc.
222 South Downey Avenue
Suite 310
Indianapolis, IN 46219
(317) 352-9226

IOWA

Iowa Affiliate, Inc.
2735 First Avenue SE
Suite 201
Cedar Rapids, IA 53402
(319) 363-5500

KANSAS

Kansas Affiliate, Inc.
3210 East Douglas
Wichita, KS 67208
(316) 684-6091

KENTUCKY

Kentucky Affiliate, Inc.
109 Hawkeegan Drive
Frankfort, KY 40601
(502) 223-2971

LOUISIANA

Louisiana Affiliate, Inc.
9420 Lindale Avenue
Suite B
Baton Rouge, LA 70815
(504) 927-7732

MAINE

Maine Affiliate, Inc.
P.O. Box 2208

Augusta, ME 04338-2208
(207) 623-2232

MARYLAND

Maryland Affiliate, Inc.
2 Reservoir Circle
Suite 203
Baltimore, MD 21208
(301) 486-5516

MASSACHUSETTS

Massachusetts Affiliate, Inc.
190 North Main Street
Natick, MA 01760
(508) 655-6900

MICHIGAN

Michigan Affiliate, Inc.
The Clausen Building, North Unit
23100 Providence Drive
Suite 400
Southfield, MI 48075
(313) 552-0480

MINNESOTA

Minnesota Affiliate, Inc.
715 Florida Avenue South
Suite 307
Minneapolis, MN 55426
(612) 593-5333

MISSISSIPPI

Mississippi Affiliate, Inc.
10 Lakeland Circle
Jackson, MS 39216
(601) 957-7878

MISSOURI

Missouri Affiliate, Inc.

P.O. Box 11
Columbia, MO 65205
(314) 443-8611

MONTANA

Montana Affiliate, Inc.
Box 2411
Great Falls, MT 59403
(406) 761-0908

NEBRASKA

Nebraska Affiliate, Inc.
2710 South 11th Street
Omaha, NE 68144
(402) 333-5556

NEVADA

Nevada Affiliate, Inc.
4045 South Spenser
Suite A-62
Las Vegas, NV 89119
(702) 369-9995

NEW HAMPSHIRE

New Hampshire Affiliate, Inc.
104 Middle Street
Manchester, NH 03105
(603) 627-9579

NEW JERSEY

New Jersey Affiliate, Inc.
P.O. Box 6423
Bridgewater, NJ 08807
(201) 725-7878

NEW MEXICO

New Mexico Affiliate, Inc.
525 San Pedro NE
Suite 101

Albuquerque, NM 87108
(505) 266-5716

NEW YORK

New York Diabetes Affiliate, Inc.
505 8th Avenue
21st Floor
New York, NY 10018
(212) 947-9707

NORTH CAROLINA

North Carolina Affiliate, Inc.
2315-A Sunset Avenue
Rocky Mount, NC 27804
(919) 937-4121

NORTH DAKOTA

North Dakota Affiliate, Inc.
P.O. Box 234
Grand Forks, ND 58206
(701) 746-4427

OHIO

Ohio Affiliate, Inc.
705-L Lakeview Plaza Boulevard
Worthington, OH 43085
(614) 436-1917

OKLAHOMA

Oklahoma Affiliate, Inc.
Warren Professional Building
6465 South Yale Avenue
Suite 519
Tulsa, OK 74136
(918) 492-3839

OREGON

Oregon Affiliate, Inc.
3607 South West Corbett Street

Portland, OR 97201
(503) 228-0849

PENNSYLVANIA

Greater Philadelphia Affiliate, Inc.
100 North 17th Street
14th Floor
Philadelphia, PA 19103
(215) 557-8070

Mid-Pennsylvania Affiliate, Inc.
2045 Westgate Drive
Suite 106
Bethlehem, PA 18017
(215) 867-6660

Western Pennsylvania Affiliate, Inc.
4617 Winthrop Street
Pittsburgh, PA 15213
(412) 682-3392

RHODE ISLAND

Rhode Island Affiliate, Inc.
Warwick Executive Park
250 Centerville Road
Warwick, RI 02886
(401) 738-5570

SOUTH CAROLINA

South Carolina Affiliate, Inc.
P.O. Box 50782
Columbia, SC 29250
(803) 799-4246

SOUTH DAKOTA

South Dakota Affiliate, Inc.
P.O. Box 659
Sioux Falls, SD 57101
(605) 335-7670

TENNESSEE

Tennessee Affiliate, Inc.
4004 Hillsboro Road
Suite B-216
Nashville, TN 37215
(615) 298-9919

TEXAS

Texas Affiliate, Inc.
8140 North Mopac
Building 1
Suite 135
Austin, TX 78759
(512) 794-8066

UTAH

Utah Affiliate, Inc.
8643 East 400 South
Salt Lake City, UT 84102
(801) 363-3024

VERMONT

Vermont Affiliate, Inc.
431 Pine Street
Burlington, VT 05401
(802) 862-3882

VIRGINIA

Virginia Affiliate, Inc.
404 8th Street NE

Suite C
Charlottesville, VA 22901
(804) 293-4953

WASHINGTON

Washington Affiliate, Inc.
3201 Fremont Avenue North
Seattle, WA 98103
(206) 632-4576

WEST VIRGINIA

West Virginia Affiliate, Inc.
1660 Duke Street
Alexandria, WV 22314
(304) 925-0161

WISCONSIN

Wisconsin Affiliate, Inc.
10721 West Capitol Drive
Milwaukee, WI 53222
(414) 464-9395

WYOMING

Wyoming Affiliate, Inc.
2908 Kelly Drive
Cheyenne, WY 82001
(307) 638-3578

FURTHER READING

Ahmed, Paul I., and N. Ahmed, eds. *Coping with Juvenile Diabetes*. Springfield, IL: Thomas, 1985.

American Diabetes Association. *Diabetes in the Family*. New York: Prentice-Hall, 1987.

Benson, William E., et al. *Diabetes and Its Ocular Complications*. Philadelphia: Saunders, 1988.

Biermann, June, and Barbara Tookey. *The Peripatetic Diabetic: Good Health, Good Times, and Good Fun for the Diabetic Who Wants to Have It All*. Los Angeles: Tarcher, 1984.

———. *Diabetics Total Health Book*. Los Angeles: Tarcher, 1988.

———. *Diabetic Woman: All Your Questions Answered*. Los Angeles: Tarcher, 1988.

Bloom, A. *Diabetes Explained*. Boston: MTP Press, 1982.

Budd, Martin L. *Low Blood Sugar: The Twentieth Century Epidemic.* New York: Sterling, 1983.

Calder, John. *Diabetes: Basic Principles of Treatment.* Portland, OR: International Specialized Book Services, 1980.

Coldwell, A. R., Jr. *Understanding Your Diabetes.* Springfield, IL: Thomas, 1978.

Covelli, Pasquale, and Melvin Wiedman. *Diabetes: Current Research and Future Directions in Management and Cure.* Jefferson, NC: McFarland, 1988.

Duncan, Theodore G. *The Diabetes Fact Book.* New York: Scribners, 1982.

Edelwich, Jerry, and Archie Brodsky. *Diabetes: Caring for Your Emotions as Well as Your Health.* Reading, MA: Addison-Wesley, 1986.

Etzwiler, Donnell, et al., eds. *Learning to Live Well with Diabetes.* Minneapolis: Diabetes Center, 1985.

Fredericks, Carlton, and Herman Goodman. *Low Blood Sugar and You.* New York: Putnam, 1969.

Jovanovic, Lois, and Charles M. Peterson. *Diabetes Self-care Method.* Rev. ed. New York: Simon & Schuster, 1984.

Jovanovic, Lois, et al. *Diabetes and Pregnancy: Teratology, Toxicity and Treatment.* New York: Praeger, 1986.

Kilo, Charles, et al. *Diabetes: The Facts that Let You Regain Control of Your Life.* New York: Wiley, 1987.

Krall, Leo, and Richard Beaser. *Joslin Diabetes Manual.* Philadelphia: Leo Febiger, 1988.

Lowe, Ernest, and Gary Arsham. *Staying Healthy with Diabetes: A Program of Individualized Health Care.* Wayzata, MN: Diabetes Center, 1988.

Maclean, Heather, and Barbara Oran. *Living with Diabetes: Personal*

Stories and Strategies for Coping. Toronto: University of Toronto Press, 1988.

Pray, Lawrence, and Richard Evans. *The Journey of a Diabetic.* New York: Simon & Schuster, 1983.

Saunders, Felicia. *Your Diabetic Child.* New York: Bantam Books, 1986.

Sims, Dorothea. *Diabetes: Reach for Health and Freedom.* St. Louis: Mosby, 1984.

Whitaker, Julian. *Reversing Diabetes.* New York: Warner Books, 1988.

GLOSSARY

acidosis excessive acidity of the bodily fluids caused by a chemical imbalance indicative of illness, as in diabetic acidosis

alpha cell one of three types of cells found in the pancreatic islets; secretes glucagon, a hormone that converts glycogen to glucose, causing blood sugar levels to increase

amino acid the building block of proteins

antibody a protein substance released into the bloodstream designed to react chemically with a specific antigen, or foreign body—a germ or another chemical—rendering it harmless; a primary molecular component of the immune system

antigen any substance, such as a toxin or bacterium, that invokes an immune response and reacts with the products of that response

atherosclerosis an arteriosclerosis characterized by the deposition of yellowish plaques and fibrous tissue in and on the innermost layer of the larger arteries

beta cell the most abundant of the three types of cells found in the pancreatic islets; secretes insulin, the protein hormone that lowers blood sugar levels

carbohydrate a member of a group of compounds that share a general biochemical structure containing carbon, hydrogen, and oxygen; includes sugars and starches

coma a state of unconsciousness from which a person cannot, in some cases, be aroused; caused by disease, injury, or poison

delta cell one of the three types of cells found in the pancreatic islets; secretes somatostatin, a hormone that inhibits glucagon and insulin

diabetes mellitus a disorder caused by the inadequate production or utilization of insulin; characterized by excessive amounts of sugar in the blood and urine, by excessive urine production, and by thirst, hunger, and loss of weight

diabetic coma the state of profound unconsciousness that occurs when uncontrolled diabetes mellitus causes severe acidosis of the blood and body tissues

endocrine gland a ductless organ that produces secretions distributed throughout the body via the bloodstream

exocrine gland an organ that releases a secretion into a canal or duct directly to specific body tissue or to the surface of the body

fat a substance containing one or more fatty acids; after glycogen, the main substance into which carbohydrates are converted for storage by the human body

gestational diabetes the onset of diabetes during pregnancy

glomerulus a cluster of blood vessels in the kidney essential to the process of blood filtration

glucagon a hormone secreted by the alpha cells of the islets of Langerhans in response to hypoglycemia, or low blood sugar; promotes the conversion of glycogen to glucose

glucose a relatively simple sugar molecule found in certain foodstuffs and in the normal blood of all animals; the principal source of energy for living organisms

glycogen a carbohydrate formed by and largely stored in the liver as a long chain of glucose molecules

hormone a chemical substance produced by one of the body's glands and carried through the blood to another organ, where it exerts a specific regulatory effect

hyperglycemia an abnormally high concentration of sugar in the blood

hypertension persistently high arterial blood pressure

hypoglycemia an abnormally low concentration of sugar in the blood

immune system a complex system of molecular and cellular components that defends the body against foreign substances and organisms

insulin a hormone produced by the beta cells of the pancreatic islets; secreted in response to elevated levels of glucose in the blood; promotes glycogen synthesis

islets of Langerhans pancreatic islets; clusters of cells that compose the endocrine portion of the pancreas; include the alpha, beta, and delta cells

ketoacidosis acidosis accompanied by the accumulation of ketones in body tissue, blood, and urine

ketone an acid compound that is the end product of fat metabolism

lymphocyte a cell produced in the lymphoid tissue that can attack foreign bodies in the blood; normally constitutes 20% to 30% of the leukocytes, or white cells, of human blood

macrophages an immune system cell, found principally in body tissue, that can engulf and destroy invading cells, protecting the body against harmful substances and infection

neuropathy a degenerative state of the nervous system or nerves

pancreas the large elongated gland situated behind the stomach and connected to the duodenum, or first part of the small intestine; secretes pancreatic juice through a duct into the duodenum for the digestion of food; as an endocrine gland, secretes insulin and glucagon for the regulation of carbohydrate metabolism

photocoagulation the condensation of proteins by the use of a highly energetic beam of light, such as a laser beam; used to treat retinal detachments

protein a compound composed of amino acids; necessary for the growth and repair of injured tissue, such as that of muscles and organs; a major source of heat and energy for the body

retinopathy any disorder of the retina

somatostatin a hormone that inhibits the secretion of insulin

triglyceride a type of fat found in most animals and vegetables; synthesized from carbohydrates and stored in animal adipose tissue

Type I diabetes mellitus insulin-dependent diabetes; disorder associated with the lack of insulin production by the beta cells

Type II diabetes mellitus non-insulin-dependent diabetes; disorder characterized by the inability of body cells to absorb the insulin that the pancreas produces; controlled through diet

uremia an excess of urea and other waste products in the blood

vitrectomy surgical removal of all or part of the vitreous humor, the clear, colorless jelly that fills the eyeball

INDEX

PICTURE CREDITS

Marjorie Little, a free-lance writer and member of the American Medical Writers Association, received her M.S. degree in sociology from the University of Pittsburgh. She is the author of the ImmunoPrimer Series, a six-part tutorial on immunology research for medical professionals, and the editor of *AIDS: You Can't Catch It Holding Hands.* She has also written *The Endocrine System* for the Chelsea House ENCYCLOPEDIA OF HEALTH series. She lives in San Francisco.

Dale C. Garell, M.D., is medical director of California Children Services, Department of Health Services, County of Los Angeles. He is also associate dean for curriculum at the University of Southern California School of Medicine and clinical professor in the Department of Pediatrics & Family Medicine at the University of Southern California School of Medicine. From 1963 to 1974, he was medical director of the Division of Adolescent Medicine at Children's Hospital in Los Angeles. Dr. Garell has served as president of the Society for Adolescent Medicine, chairman of the youth committee of the American Academy of Pediatrics, and as a forum member of the White House Conference on Children (1970) and White House Conference on Youth (1971). He has also been a member of the editorial board of the *American Journal of Diseases of Children.*

C. Everett Koop, M.D., Sc.D., is former Surgeon General, deputy assistant secretary for health, and director of the Office of International Health of the U.S. Public Health Service. A pediatric surgeon with an international reputation, he was previously surgeon-in-chief of Children's Hospital of Philadelphia and professor of pediatric surgery and pediatrics at the University of Pennsylvania. Dr. Koop is the author of more than 175 articles and books on the practice of medicine. He has served as surgery editor of the *Journal of Clinical Pediatrics* and editor-in-chief of the *Journal of Pediatric Surgery.* Dr. Koop has received nine honorary degrees and numerous other awards, including the Denis Brown Gold Medal of the British Association of Paediatric Surgeons, the William E. Ladd Gold Medal of the American Academy of Pediatrics, and the Copernicus Medal of the Surgical Society of Poland. He is a chevalier of the French Legion of Honor and a member of the Royal College of Surgeons, London.